BAKING HACKS

Pillsbury

BAKING HACKS

FUN AND INVENTIVE RECIPES WITH REFRIGERATED DOUGH

Houghton Mifflin Harcourt
Boston · New York · 2018

GENERAL MILLS

Global Business Solutions Director:
Heather Polen

Global Business Solutions Manager:
Maja Qamar

Executive Editor: Cathy Swanson Wheaton

Photography: General Mills Photography
Studios and Image Library

HOUGHTON MIFFLIN HARCOURT

Editor-in-Chief: Deb Brody

Executive Editor: Anne Ficklen

Editorial Associate: Sarah Kwak

Managing Editor: Marina Padakis

Production Editor: Helen Seachrist

Cover Design: Tai Blanche

Interior Design and Layout: Tai Blanche

Senior Production Coordinator:
Kimberly Kiefer

Library of Congress Cataloging-in-Publication Data
Names: Pillsbury Company.
Title: Pillsbury baking hacks: fun and inventive recipes with refrigerated dough /
    [Phillsbury editors].
Description: Boston: Houghton Mifflin Harcourt, 2018.
Identifiers: LCCN 2017058456 (print) | LCCN 2018003381 (ebook) |
    ISBN 9781328503817 (ebook) | ISBN 9781328497857 (trade paper)
Subjects: LCSH: Baking. | Cooking (Bread) | Dough. | Cooking, American. |
    LCGFT: Cookbooks.
Classification: LCC TX765 (ebook) | LCC TX765 .P51933 2018 (print) |
    DDC 641.8⅕—dc23
LC record available at https://lccn.loc.gov/2017058456

Manufactured in China

C&C 10 9 8 7 6 5 4 3 2 1

Cover photos: Dill Pickle Pull-Apart (page 127); Lemon Cookie and Raspberry Yogurt Pops
(page 215); BBQ Mac-and-Cheese Appetizer Pizza (page 55); German Chocolate–Coconut
Baked Doughnuts (page 68)

Home of the Pillsbury Bake-Off® Contest

Pillsbury

For more great recipes, visit
pillsbury.com

DEAR BAKER,

We know family comes first at your house—you want to feed your bunch well and enjoy eating together. But like us, you don't always have a lot of time to spend in the kitchen. Let us help! *Pillsbury Baking Hacks* gives you great ways to get meals on the table, which both you and your family will love.

This book is loaded with hacks—tricks we've learned to cut prep time, leaving you with more time for family fun! Making meals at home is easy with these clever recipes. (We challenge you to find anyone that can their resist their yumminess!)

Be inspired with the customizability you can have with Pillsbury dough! Scrumptious sweet breads to wake the sleepyheads, crazy-simple weeknight dinners to help you survive those impossibly busy nights, as well as appetizers and desserts that bring on the wows! Look for the features that each highlight one type of recipe—with 3 completely different variations. You'll also love the ingenious, no-fuss food ideas to make your own creations with Pillsbury dough products.

Make it easy, make it fun with Pillsbury!

The Pillsbury™ Editors

CONTENTS

FEATURES

IT'S ALL ABOUT THE HACKS

WHAT IS A HACK?

Feeding your busy family, whipping up a party appetizer that's sure to be a hit or bringing the perfect dessert to a potluck can be daunting. What you need are some terrific shortcuts in your cooking arsenal. Hacks are just that—clever shortcuts. Pillsbury™ dough products are great hacks in and of themselves. They get you to hot, homemade deliciousness faster than starting from flour.

WE'VE LAYERED THE HACKS

At first glance, you might think this is just an ordinary cookbook, but it's not! Pillsbury biscuits aren't the only thing with a lot of layers. We've loaded up the layers of hacks for you in this book to help you solve all those times when you need to whip up something fast. Look at all the help you're getting in the kitchen:

TRADITIONAL HACKS All the recipes are hacks because they start with a Pillsbury refrigerated dough product, saving you time in the kitchen.

RECIPE HACKS These features show you twists on a specific type of Pillsbury dough recipe. The clever variations give you options and inspiration to create your own recipes using what you have on hand or your favorite ingredients!

PRODUCT HACKS Focus on a Pillsbury dough product and see the possibilities! We'll show you easy and creative ways to use it. (We were thinking outside the "can" for these!)

KITCHEN HACKS These are our favorite cooking hacks from the test kitchens, which we love to share. They save time and make your kitchen experiences a breeze. Look for these sprinkled throughout the book.

WE'VE KEPT IT SIMPLE

We know you're looking for ways to get food on the table without spending all day in the kitchen. Look for the recipes with these icons: 3-INGREDIENT, 5-INGREDIENT and QUICK PREP. These super-simple recipes are surprisingly perfect for your family or to serve to company, and you'll love how fast they come together!

When counting ingredients to see if they make the mark, we didn't include regular salt, pepper, water, cooking spray if used to grease a pan, or flour if used just to dust the work surface. Most likely, you have these on hand and won't need to make a special trip to the store for them, as you might for other ingredients.

Recipes that need only 20 minutes or less of prep time make for easy work in the kitchen. Prep time is active preparation, where you need to be working with or paying close attention to the food (not things like baking or refrigerating, where you can walk away and do something else).

DOUGH DOS

Working with refrigerated dough is a snap when you know these tips:

- Store dough on a shelf in the refrigerator. Temperatures in the door or a crisper may be too warm or cool to store the dough properly.

- Keep dough refrigerated and in the package or can until you are ready to open and use it. Don't allow it to sit at room temperature very long or it can become warm and sticky, making it harder to work with.

- Keep your dough products in the refrigerator—don't freeze them. When frozen, the leavening will be inactivated, causing the dough not to rise. Cookie dough and pie crust are exceptions. Look on the package for directions on how to freeze these products.

- Always use dough by the expiration date on the end of the can or on the package. Exceptions are cookie dough and pie crust, which can be refrigerated up to 2 months.

- For the dough to bake correctly, always preheat the oven and bake on the middle rack of your oven unless the recipe indicates otherwise.

- Serve refrigerated dough products warm from the oven unless the recipe indicates otherwise.

- Dough products should not be cooked in the microwave oven as they will not rise or bake properly or brown.

EMERGENCY SUBSTITUTIONS

Sometimes you just don't have the right ingredient or time to run to the store. Look here for substitutions to use in a pinch:

FOOD	AMOUNT	REPLACE WITH
Baking powder	1 teaspoon	½ teaspoon cream of tartar + ¼ teaspoon baking soda
Bread crumbs	½ cup	1 slice fresh bread processed in food processor into crumbs
Brown sugar	1 cup	1 cup granulated sugar + 2 tablespoons molasses
Buttermilk	1 cup	1 tablespoon lemon juice or vinegar + enough milk to make 1 cup
Chocolate	Unsweetened baking (1 ounce)	3 tablespoons baking cocoa + 1 tablespoon shortening
	Semisweet chips (1 cup)	6 ounces unsweetened baking chocolate + 1 tablespoon sugar OR 1 tablespoon baking cocoa + 2 tablespoons sugar + 2 teaspoons shortening
Chocolate wafer crumbs	1½ cups	27 cookies
Cornstarch	1 tablespoon	2 tablespoons all-purpose flour
Graham cracker crumbs	1½ cups	21 squares processed in food processor into crumbs
Ground beef	1 pound	1 pound ground turkey or chicken
Pizza sauce	Any amount	Pasta sauce
Sour cream	1 cup	1 cup plain, full- or lowfat yogurt (do not use fat-free in baked goods)
Tomato sauce	15-ounce can	1 can (6 ounces) tomato paste + 1½ cans water
Yeast	1 package (.25 ounce)	2¼ teaspoons regular or active dry yeast
Yogurt (plain)	1 cup	1 cup sour cream

APPETIZERS

EASY BAKED MOZZARELLA BITES

PREP TIME: 20 Minutes | **START TO FINISH:** 35 Minutes | 24 bites

1   can Pillsbury refrigerated crescent dough sheet

8   mozzarella sticks (from 12-oz package), unwrapped. cut crosswise into thirds

3   tablespoons butter, melted

⅔   cup Italian-style panko crispy bread crumbs

1   Heat oven to 375°F. Unroll dough on cutting board; starting at center, press into 12x8-inch rectangle. Using pizza cutter or sharp knife, cut rectangle into 6 rows by 4 rows to make 24 (2-inch) squares.

2   Place mozzarella stick in center of each rectangle. Bring dough up and around cheese sticks; press edges to seal.

3   Pour melted butter into small bowl. Place bread crumbs in another small bowl. Dip each stick into butter; shake off excess. Roll in bread crumbs to coat. Place about 1 inch apart on ungreased large cookie sheet.

4   Bake 11 to 13 minutes or until golden brown. Serve warm.

1 Bite: Calories 80; Total Fat 4.5g (Saturated Fat 2.5g, Trans Fat 0g); Cholesterol 10mg; Sodium 200mg; Total Carbohydrate 7g (Dietary Fiber 0g); Protein 3g **Exchanges:** ½ Starch, 1 Fat **Carbohydrate Choices:** ½

KITCHEN SECRETS

◆ Change up the flavor of these crunchy two-bite snacks by using other varieties of cheese sticks.

◆ You can substitute 1 can Pillsbury refrigerated crescent dinner rolls (8 rolls) for the dough sheet. Unroll dough and firmly press perforations to seal. Continue as directed.

SERVE IT UP

◆ Serve with warm marinara sauce or ranch dressing—or both. Yum!

KITCHEN HACK

SOFTEN CREAM CHEESE

Remove the wrapper from the cream cheese or remove it from the tub, and place it in a microwavable glass bowl. Microwave on Medium (50%) 45 seconds to 1 minute 30 seconds.

SALTED BEER PRETZEL PIGSKIN BITES

PREP TIME: 25 Minutes | **START TO FINISH:** 45 Minutes | 24 bites

1   can Pillsbury refrigerated crescent dinner rolls (8 rolls)

24   cocktail-size smoked link sausages (from 14-oz package)

1   egg

1   can or bottle (12 oz) Pilsner beer

¼   cup baking soda

⅛   teaspoon coarse (kosher or sea) salt

Yellow mustard, from a squeeze bottle

1. Heat oven to 375°F. Line large cookie sheet with cooking parchment paper.

2. Separate crescent dough into 8 triangles on cutting board. Cut each triangle lengthwise into 3 narrow triangles. Place 1 sausage on shortest side of each triangle. Roll up, rolling to opposite point.

3. In small bowl, beat egg and 1 tablespoon of the beer with whisk until thoroughly blended; set aside.

4. In large microwavable bowl, microwave remaining beer uncovered on High 1 minute 45 seconds or until hot. Gradually add baking soda, stirring until baking soda is completely dissolved. Using metal tongs, dip each rolled crescent, one at a time, into beer and baking soda mixture. Place on cooling rack. Let stand at room temperature about 5 minutes.

5. Brush crescents with beer and egg mixture, and sprinkle with coarse salt. Carefully place on cookie sheet.

6. Bake 12 to 15 minutes or until tops are deep golden brown. Cool 2 minutes. Onto each bite, squeeze 1 line of mustard crosswise and 3 lines lengthwise to make laces of football. Serve warm.

1 Bite: Calories 70; Total Fat 4.5g (Saturated Fat 2g, Trans Fat 0g); Cholesterol 15mg; Sodium 810mg; Total Carbohydrate 4g (Dietary Fiber 0g); Protein 2g **Exchanges:** ½ Other Carbohydrate, 1 Fat **Carbohydrate Choices:** 0

KITCHEN SECRET

◆ Adding baking soda to the beer helps transform the crescent into a pretzel.

ADD A GARNISH

◆ Perfect for game day! Use your favorite mustard, sour cream or softened cream cheese to make football laces on these irresistible appetizers. Transfer it to a small resealable food-storage bag, then cut off a small corner of the bag to make it easy to squeeze onto top of each appetizer.

CHEESY MUSHROOM CRESCENT PUFFS

PREP TIME: 30 Minutes | **START TO FINISH:** 1 Hour 5 Minutes | **32 puffs**

4 cups finely chopped mushrooms (from two 8-oz packages)

1½ teaspoons chopped fresh thyme leaves

¼ teaspoon salt

1 cup finely shredded Italian cheese blend (4 oz)

1 can Pillsbury refrigerated crescent dough sheet

1 tablespoon all-purpose flour

1 Heat oven to 375°F. Line 2 (15x10x1-inch) pans with cooking parchment paper; spray with cooking spray.

2 Spray 10-inch skillet with cooking spray. Add mushrooms; cook over medium-high heat 5 to 7 minutes, stirring occasionally, until tender and most of moisture is released. Stir in thyme and salt. Remove from heat. Cool 5 minutes.

3 In large bowl, stir mushrooms and cheese until well blended.

4 Unroll dough on cutting board. Sprinkle each side with 1½ teaspoons flour. With pizza cutter or sharp knife, cut dough into ¼ inch pieces. Mix dough pieces into mushroom mixture in small amounts until well blended.

5 Shape mushroom mixture into 32 (1¼-inch) balls. Place on pans. Bake 16 to 18 minutes or until golden brown.

1 Puff: Calories 45; Total Fat 2g (Saturated Fat 1g, Trans Fat 0g); Cholesterol 0mg; Sodium 115mg; Total Carbohydrate 5g (Dietary Fiber 0g); Protein 1g **Exchanges:** ½ Starch, ½ Fat **Carbohydrate Choices:** ½

KITCHEN SECRETS

◆ For a more woodsy flavor, try cremini mushrooms.

◆ You can use 1 can Pillsbury refrigerated crescent dinner rolls (8 rolls) instead of the dough sheet. Unroll dough and firmly press perforations to seal. Continue as directed.

SERVE IT UP

◆ Serve with your favorite flavor aioli, ranch dressing or marinara sauce for dipping.

CHEESY CHORIZO CRESCENT BITES

PREP TIME: 30 Minutes | START TO FINISH: 45 Minutes | 24 bites

½ lb bulk chorizo sausage

½ cup chive & onion cream cheese spread (from 8-oz container)

½ cup shredded Cheddar cheese (2 oz)

1 can Pillsbury refrigerated crescent dough sheet

1 Heat oven to 375°F. In 10-inch nonstick skillet, cook sausage over medium-high heat 4 to 5 minutes, stirring frequently, until sausage is no longer pink; drain and cool 5 minutes. In medium bowl, mix sausage, cream cheese spread and Cheddar cheese.

2 Unroll dough on cutting board. Starting at center, press dough into 12x8-inch rectangle. With pizza cutter or sharp knife, cut into 6 rows by 4 rows to make 24 squares.

3 Divide sausage mixture evenly in center of each dough square. Bring four corners together to overlap slightly in center at top of each bundle. Twist and pinch to seal, leaving small gaps between seams. Place on large ungreased cookie sheet.

4 Bake 11 to 15 minutes or until golden brown. Serve warm.

1 Bite: Calories 70; Total Fat 4.5g (Saturated Fat 2g, Trans Fat 0g); Cholesterol 10mg; Sodium 150mg; Total Carbohydrate 5g (Dietary Fiber 0g); Protein 2g **Exchanges:** ½ Starch, 1 Fat **Carbohydrate Choices:** ½

KITCHEN SECRETS

◆ Chorizo varies in flavor and type by region. You may need to drain chorizo after cooking. We used a more traditional Mexican variety in our testing.

◆ You can substitute 1 can Pillsbury refrigerated crescent dinner rolls (8 rolls) for the dough sheet. Unroll dough and firmly press perforations to seal. Continue as directed.

ADD A GARNISH

◆ Top each chorizo bite with sour cream, chopped fresh cilantro and sliced green onions.

EASY JALAPEÑO POPPERS

PREP TIME: 10 Minutes | **START TO FINISH:** 30 Minutes | 16 poppers

1 can Pillsbury refrigerated crescent dinner rolls (8 rolls)

8 small jalapeño chiles

1 container (8 oz) garden vegetable cream cheese spread

1 Heat oven to 375°F. Separate dough into 8 triangles. Cut each triangle lengthwise into 2 narrow triangles.

2 Cut chiles in half lengthwise; remove seeds. Spoon cream cheese spread into chile halves.

3 Place 1 stuffed chile half on shortest side of each triangle. Roll up, starting at shortest side of triangle and rolling to opposite point; place point side down on ungreased cookie sheet.

4 Bake 14 to 18 minutes or until poppers are deep golden brown.

1 Popper: Calories 90; Total Fat 7g (Saturated Fat 3.5g, Trans Fat 0g); Cholesterol 15mg; Sodium 180mg; Total Carbohydrate 7g (Dietary Fiber 0g); Protein 1g **Exchanges:** ½ Starch, 1½ Fat **Carbohydrate Choices:** ½

KITCHEN SECRETS

Be sure to handle jalapeños carefully! The oils that get on your hands can cause some burning, especially if you rub your eyes. If possible, use food-safe plastic gloves when working with the chiles—you can find them at the pharmacy.

Stir a couple slices of cooked and crumbled bacon into the cream cheese mixture before stuffing the jalapeños.

KITCHEN HACK

DISSOLVE HONEY CRYSTALS

Leave the honey in the jar but remove the lid. Microwave ½ to 1 cup 45 seconds to 1½ minutes, stirring about every 30 seconds or until crystals dissolve.

Clockwise from top left:
Mac-and-Cheese Pepperoni
Poppers (page 22)
Parmesan Pretzel Poppers with
Spinach Sriracha Dip (page 23)
Easy Jalapeño Poppers (left)

MAC-AND-CHEESE PEPPERONI POPPERS

PREP TIME: 20 Minutes | **START TO FINISH:** 40 Minutes | 16 poppers

1 can Pillsbury Grands!™ Flaky Layers refrigerated buttermilk biscuits (8 biscuits)

1 cup prepared macaroni and cheese

⅓ cup mini pepperoni slices (from 5-oz package)

3 tablespoons chopped green onions with tops

1 tablespoon butter, melted

1 Heat oven to 375°F. Spray large cookie sheet with cooking spray.

2 Separate dough into 8 biscuits; separate each into 2 layers. Using fingers, press each biscuit layer into 3-inch round. If sticky, dust fingers lightly with flour.

3 In small bowl, combine macaroni and cheese, pepperoni and 2 tablespoons of the green onions.

4 For each popper, place 1 tablespoon macaroni mixture in center of dough round. Wrap dough around filling, pinching edges to seal, forming a ball.

5 Arrange balls on cookie sheet sealed side down, about 2 inches apart. Brush with melted butter and sprinkle with remaining 1 tablespoon green onions.

6 Bake 15 to 20 minutes or until golden brown. Serve warm.

1 Popper: Calories 130; Total Fat 6g (Saturated Fat 2.5g, Trans Fat 0g); Cholesterol 5mg; Sodium 310mg; Total Carbohydrate 16g (Dietary Fiber 0g); Protein 3g **Exchanges:** 1 Starch, 1 Fat **Carbohydrate Choices:** 1

KITCHEN SECRETS

If you can't find the mini pepperoni, chop regular pepperoni slices into small pieces.

These appetizers are a fun way to use leftover macaroni and cheese. Warm the macaroni and cheese before adding the pepperoni and onions; it will be easier to mix.

If you want to make sandwiches rather than appetizers, don't separate the biscuits. In the center of each biscuit, place about 2 tablespoons of the macaroni mixture. Continue as directed.

PARMESAN PRETZEL POPPERS WITH SPINACH–SRIRACHA DIP

PREP TIME: 30 Minutes | **START TO FINISH:** 3 Hours | **16 servings**

DIP

- 1 package (10 oz) frozen spinach, thawed, squeezed to drain
- 1 package (8 oz) cream cheese, softened
- 1 package (8 oz) sliced American cheese, chopped (2 cups)
- 1 can (10 oz) diced tomatoes with green chiles, undrained
- 2 to 3 teaspoons Sriracha sauce

PRETZELS

- 3 cups water
- 2 tablespoons baking soda
- 2 teaspoons grated Parmesan cheese
- 1 teaspoon coarse garlic powder with parsley
- 1 can Pillsbury refrigerated original breadsticks (12 breadsticks)
- 1 tablespoon butter, melted

1. Spray 1½- to 2-quart slow cooker with cooking spray. Add dip ingredients to slow cooker; stir until well blended. Cover; cook 2 to 3 hours or until hot and bubbly.

2. Meanwhile, heat oven to 375°F. Line large cookie sheet with cooking parchment paper.

3. In 10-inch skillet, heat water and soda to boiling over high heat. In small bowl, combine Parmesan cheese and garlic powder until mixed; set aside.

4. Unroll dough on cutting board; cut each breadstick into 48 (1-inch) pieces. Carefully place 5 to 6 of the dough pieces into boiling water; cook 15 seconds on each side. Using slotted spoon, place dough pieces on cookie sheet 1 inch apart. Repeat with remaining dough pieces. Brush with melted butter; sprinkle with Parmesan mixture.

5. Bake 12 to 14 minutes or until golden brown. Remove poppers from cookie sheet. Serve warm with dip. Store leftover dip covered in refrigerator.

1 Serving (3 Poppers and 2 Tablespoons Dip): Calories 120; Total Fat 6g (Saturated Fat 3g, Trans Fat 0g); Cholesterol 15mg; Sodium 310mg; Total Carbohydrate 11g (Dietary Fiber 0g); Protein 3g **Exchanges:** 1 Starch, 1 Fat **Carbohydrate Choices:** 1

KITCHEN SECRETS

You can make the Sriracha dip ahead of time, then cover and refrigerate. Simply reheat dip in slow cooker by cooking covered on Low heat setting 1 to 2 hours.

To quickly thaw spinach, cut a small slit in center of pouch. Microwave on High 2 to 3 minutes or until thawed. Remove spinach from pouch; squeeze dry with paper towels.

Small slow cookers, 1½- to 2-quart, often offer only one heat setting. If you have one that has both Low and High heat settings, use the Low heat setting.

SERVE IT UP

These pretzel poppers are a great appetizer for any party. This dip recipe makes more than you need for the poppers, but don't worry about leftovers. Set it out with tortilla chips and crackers, and watch it disappear!

ROASTED TOMATO–GOAT CHEESE TARTS

PREP TIME: 30 Minutes | **START TO FINISH:** 45 Minutes | 15 tarts

2 oz crumbled goat cheese (½ cup)

1 tablespoon honey

1 teaspoon dried thyme leaves

1 tablespoon plus 2 teaspoons olive oil

1 medium sweet onion, halved, sliced (2½ cups)

1 can Pillsbury refrigerated crescent dough sheet

2 plum (Roma) tomatoes, thinly sliced

1 Heat oven to 400°F. Lightly spray large cookie sheet with cooking spray. In small bowl, combine goat cheese, honey and ½ teaspoon of the thyme; set aside.

2 In 10-inch skillet, heat 1 tablespoon olive oil over medium-high heat. Stir in onions to coat with oil. Cook uncovered 10 minutes, stirring every 2 to 3 minutes, or until golden brown.

3 Unroll dough on work surface. Starting at center, gently pat into 14x8-inch rectangle. Using 2½-inch round cookie cutter, cut into 15 rounds, rerolling if necessary. Place rounds ½ inch apart on cookie sheet.

4 Gently spread about 1 teaspoon goat cheese mixture onto each round. Top with onion and tomato slices. Drizzle with 2 teaspoons olive oil. Sprinkle with remaining ½ teaspoon thyme.

5 Bake 10 to 13 minutes or until crust is golden brown. Immediately remove from cookie sheet. Serve warm.

1 Tart: Calories 70; Total Fat 4g (Saturated Fat 1.5g, Trans Fat 0g); Cholesterol 0mg; Sodium 90mg; Total Carbohydrate 7g (Dietary Fiber 0g); Protein 1g **Exchanges:** ½ Other Carbohydrate, 1 Fat **Carbohydrate Choices:** ½

KITCHEN SECRETS

◆ Sweet onions are milder than regular yellow or white onions. Sweet varieties include Vidalia, Walla Walla and Maui onions.

◆ If the dough sticks to the cookie cutter, dip it into flour before cutting the rounds.

◆ If you like, sprinkle tarts with salt and pepper before baking.

BACON-CREAM CHEESE CRESCENT CUPS

PREP TIME: 25 Minutes | START TO FINISH: 40 Minutes | 24 cups

1 can Pillsbury refrigerated crescent dough sheet

1 cup finely shredded Mexican cheese blend (4 oz)

4 oz (half of 8-oz package) cream cheese, softened

2 tablespoons chopped seeded serrano chiles

3 slices bacon, crisply cooked, crumbled

1 Heat oven to 375°F. Unroll dough on work surface. Starting at center, press into 12x9-inch rectangle. With pizza cutter or sharp knife, cut into 6 rows by 4 rows to make 24 squares. Press 1 square in bottom and up side of each of 24 ungreased nonstick mini muffin cups.

2 In medium bowl, mix Mexican cheese blend, cream cheese, chiles and bacon until well blended. Spoon 1 rounded teaspoonful cream cheese mixture into each cup.

3 Bake 8 to 12 minutes or until golden brown. Cool 2 minutes; remove from pan to serving platter. Serve warm.

1 Cup: Calories 70; Total Fat 4.5g (Saturated Fat 2g, Trans Fat 0g); Cholesterol 10mg; Sodium 125mg; Total Carbohydrate 5g (Dietary Fiber 0g); Protein 2g **Exchanges:** ½ Starch, 1 Fat **Carbohydrate Choices:** ½

KITCHEN SECRETS

◆ Keep dough in the refrigerator until you're ready to use it. Cold dough is much easier to work with than warm dough.

◆ Can't find serrano chiles? Substitute jalapeño chiles for a milder flavor.

◆ You can substitute 1 can Pillsbury refrigerated crescent dinner rolls (8 rolls) for the dough sheet. Unroll dough and firmly press perforations to seal. Continue as directed.

ADD A GARNISH

◆ Quarter 6 cherry tomatoes. Garnish each crescent cup with 1 tomato wedge and 1 cilantro sprig.

RASPBERRY-JALAPEÑO BRIE CUPS

PREP TIME: 20 Minutes | **START TO FINISH:** 40 Minutes | 24 cups

1   can Pillsbury refrigerated crescent dough sheet

⅓   cup seedless raspberry-jalapeño preserves

4   oz Brie cheese, cut into 24 pieces

1. Heat oven to 375°F. Spray 24 mini muffin cups with cooking spray.

2. Unroll dough on cutting board; cut into 6 rows by 4 rows to make 24 squares. Press 1 square into bottom and up side of each muffin cup. Spoon about ½ teaspoon preserves into each cup.

3. Bake 8 to 12 minutes or until light golden brown. Remove from oven. Place 1 piece of the Brie in each cup. Bake 2 to 3 minutes longer or until cheese is soft. Cool in cups 5 minutes; remove from muffin cups.

1 Cup: Calories 60; Total Fat 2.5g (Saturated Fat 1g, Trans Fat 0g); Cholesterol 0mg; Sodium 105mg; Total Carbohydrate 8g (Dietary Fiber 0g); Protein 1g **Exchanges:** ½ Starch, ½ Fat **Carbohydrate Choices:** ½

KITCHEN SECRET

◆ These sweet and spicy cups are perfect for any BBQ, game day or holiday party.

ADD A GARNISH

◆ To make these crescent cups special, top each cup with 1 small fresh raspberry and chopped chives after melting the Brie.

KITCHEN HACK

KEEP-IT-GREEN AVOCADOS

Help keep guacamole from browning by tossing cut avocado with a little lime or lemon juice before adding other ingredients.

CHEESEBURGER MEATLOAF CUPS

PREP TIME: 20 Minutes | **START TO FINISH:** 35 Minutes | 24 cups

1	can Pillsbury refrigerated crescent dough sheet
½	lb lean (at least 85%) ground beef
½	cup finely shredded extra-sharp Cheddar cheese (2 oz)
1	tablespoon finely chopped onion
3	tablespoons ketchup
1	teaspoon yellow mustard
¼	teaspoon salt

1. Heat oven to 375°F. Spray 24 mini muffin cups with cooking spray.

2. Unroll dough on cutting board. Starting at center, press into 12x8-inch rectangle. Cut dough into 6 rows by 4 rows to make 24 squares. Gently press 1 square into bottom and up side of each muffin cup.

3. In medium bowl, stir together ground beef, Cheddar cheese, onion, 1 tablespoon of the ketchup, the mustard and salt until well mixed.

4. Shape mixture into 24 (1-inch) balls. Press each ball into muffin cup, pressing to flatten top. Brush tops of meatloaf mixture with remaining 2 tablespoons ketchup.

5. Bake 10 to 15 minutes or until meat is no longer pink in center and thermometer inserted into center reads 160°F. Immediately remove from muffin cups. Serve warm.

1 Cup: Calories 60; Total Fat 2.5g (Saturated Fat 1g, Trans Fat 0g); Cholesterol 10mg; Sodium 140mg; Total Carbohydrate 5g (Dietary Fiber 0g); Protein 2g **Exchanges:** ½ Starch, ½ Fat **Carbohydrate Choices:** ½

KITCHEN SECRET

◆ For a crispier cup, prebake the cups 5 to 7 minutes before adding the meatloaf mixture.

ADD A GARNISH

◆ Garnish with additional mustard, shredded lettuce or other favorite cheeseburger toppings.

KITCHEN HACK

EASY JUICING

Get more juice from a lemon or lime by rolling it on counter with palm of hand, using some pressure, before juicing.

Clockwise from top:
Green Olive and
Parmesan Pinwheels
(right)
Feta-Spinach
Pinwheels (page 34)
Buffalo Chicken
Sausage Pinwheels
(page 35)

GREEN OLIVE AND PARMESAN PINWHEELS

PREP TIME: 15 Minutes | **START TO FINISH:** 30 Minutes | 16 pinwheels

- 1 can Pillsbury refrigerated crescent dough sheet
- ⅓ cup finely chopped pimiento-stuffed green olives
- ¼ cup grated Parmesan cheese
- ¼ teaspoon seasoned pepper

1 Heat oven to 350°F. Spray large cookie sheet with cooking spray. Unroll dough on cutting board.

2 In small bowl, combine olives, Parmesan cheese and pepper. Spread mixture over dough to within ¼ inch of edges.

3 Starting with one long side, roll up dough sheet; press seam to seal. With sharp serrated knife, cut roll into 16 slices. On cookie sheet, place slices cut side down about 1 inch apart.

4 Bake 12 to 15 minutes or until edges are golden brown. Immediately remove from cookie sheet. Serve warm.

1 Pinwheel: Calories 50; Total Fat 2.5g (Saturated Fat 1g, Trans Fat 0g); Cholesterol 0mg; Sodium 190mg; Total Carbohydrate 7g (Dietary Fiber 0g); Protein 1g **Exchanges:** ½ Starch, ½ Fat **Carbohydrate Choices:** ½

KITCHEN SECRET

Use your favorite type of pitted sliced olives in this appetizer, or combine two different types of olives.

SERVE IT UP

If you like, serve these pinwheels with a super simple dip of warmed pizza sauce or your favorite marinara sauce.

ADD A GARNISH

Sprinkle with additional seasoned pepper.

KITCHEN HACK

NO-FUSS BACON

Let your oven cook the bacon so you don't have to stand and watch it. Line a 15x10x1-inch pan with foil. Cook the bacon in a single layer on a wire cooling rack in the pan at 350°F 20 minutes. Turn bacon; cook 10 to 15 minutes longer or until crisp.

FETA-SPINACH PINWHEELS

PREP TIME: 10 Minutes | **START TO FINISH:** 30 Minutes | 16 pinwheels

1 can Pillsbury refrigerated crescent dough sheet

1 container (4 oz) crumbled basil and tomato feta cheese

½ cup squeezed frozen (thawed) chopped spinach (from 9-oz box)

1 Heat oven to 350°F. Spray large baking sheet with cooking spray.

2 Unroll dough on cutting board. Starting at center, press into 12x8-inch rectangle. Sprinkle with cheese and spinach.

3 Starting with one long side, roll up rectangle; press edge to seal. With sharp serrated knife, cut into 16 slices; place cut side down on cookie sheet about 2 inches apart.

4 Bake 14 to 18 minutes or until edges are golden brown. Immediately remove from cookie sheet. Serve warm.

1 Pinwheel: Calories 70; Total Fat 3.5g (Saturated Fat 1.5g, Trans Fat 0g); Cholesterol 5mg; Sodium 200mg; Total Carbohydrate 7g (Dietary Fiber 0g); Protein 2g **Exchanges:** ½ Starch, ½ Fat **Carbohydrate Choices:** ½

KITCHEN SECRET

To remove excess moisture from thawed frozen spinach, drain it in a mesh strainer. Then place several layers of paper towels on cutting board. Place spinach on towels; roll up and squeeze out additional moisture. Before adding to recipe, separate spinach with fingers or a fork to avoid clumps.

ADD A GARNISH

Dress up this simple recipe by sprinkling thinly sliced fresh basil over pinwheels.

KITCHEN HACK

QUICK CUTTING

Use a pizza cutter to cut crescent dough sheets quickly into squares for appetizers.

BUFFALO CHICKEN SAUSAGE PINWHEELS

PREP TIME: 20 Minutes | **START TO FINISH:** 40 Minutes | **16 pinwheels**

PINWHEELS

- 1 can Pillsbury refrigerated crescent dough sheet
- 2 oz cream cheese, softened (from 8-oz package)
- ¼ cup crumbled blue cheese (1 oz)
- ¼ cup shredded sharp Cheddar cheese (2 oz)
- 1 tablespoon Buffalo wing sauce
- 1 link (3 oz) fully cooked Italian-style chicken sausage (from 12-oz package), finely chopped
- 2 tablespoons chopped green onions with tops (2 medium)

DIP

- 1 cup ranch dressing
- 1 tablespoon Buffalo wing sauce

1. Heat oven to 350°F. Line large cookie sheet with cooking parchment paper. Unroll dough on cutting board.

2. In small bowl, beat cheeses and 1 tablespoon Buffalo sauce with electric mixer on medium speed 1 to 2 minutes or until well mixed. Spread cream cheese mixture on dough to within ¼ inch of edges. Sprinkle with chicken sausage and green onion.

3. Starting with one long side, roll up dough; press edge to seal. Place seam side down. With sharp serrated knife, cut into 16 slices; place cut side down on cookie sheet about 2 inches apart.

4. Bake 15 to 20 minutes or until edges are golden brown. Immediately remove from cookie sheet.

5. Meanwhile, in small bowl, stir dressing and 1 tablespoon Buffalo chicken sauce until well blended. Serve warm with dip.

1 Pinwheel: Calories 150; Total Fat 12g (Saturated Fat 3.5g, Trans Fat 0g); Cholesterol 15mg; Sodium 360mg; Total Carbohydrate 8g (Dietary Fiber 0g); Protein 3g **Exchanges:** ½ Starch, 2½ Fat **Carbohydrate Choices:** ½

SERVE IT UP

These pinwheels make a great game-day appetizer. Serve with carrot and celery sticks or other vegetable dippers.

ADD A GARNISH

For extra color and texture, sprinkle pinwheels with 1 tablespoon chopped green onion before baking, and garnish dip with sliced green onions.

KITCHEN HACK

SIMPLE SEPARATION

Using cold eggs right out of the refrigerator is the easiest way to separate yolks from whites.

MEATBALL MUMMY CRESCENT BITES

PREP TIME: 15 Minutes | **START TO FINISH:** 30 Minutes | 10 servings

1   can Pillsbury refrigerated crescent dinner rolls (8 rolls)

20 frozen cooked meatballs, thawed

Ketchup or mustard

1   Heat oven to 375°F. Line work surface with cooking parchment paper. Unroll dough on cutting board; press perforations to seal. Cut into 4 rectangles.

2   With sharp knife or pizza cutter, cut each rectangle lengthwise into 10 pieces, making a total of 40 pieces of dough.

3   Wrap 2 pieces of dough around each meatball to look like "bandages," stretching dough slightly to cover meatballs.

4   Separate "bandages" near one end to show meatball "face." On ungreased large cookie sheet, place wrapped meatballs.

5   Bake 13 to 17 minutes or until dough is light golden brown and meatballs are hot. With ketchup and mustard, draw "eyes" on each mummy bite.

1 Serving (2 Bites): Calories 150; Total Fat 9g (Saturated Fat 3.5g, Trans Fat 0g); Cholesterol 30mg; Sodium 340mg; Total Carbohydrate 12g (Dietary Fiber 0g); Protein 6g **Exchanges:** ½ Starch, ½ Other Carbohydrate, ½ High-Fat Meat, 1 Fat **Carbohydrate Choices:** 1

KITCHEN SECRET

◆ You can substitute 1 can Pillsbury refrigerated crescent dough sheet for the crescent rolls if you prefer. Just unroll and cut as directed.

SERVE IT UP

◆ Serve these frightfully fun appetizers with warm marinara sauce.

KITCHEN HACK

CLEVER CUTTING

Don't have cookie cutters the right size to cut your dough? Use items around your kitchen that are the size called for in the recipe, such as an empty soup can, a coffee cup or a plate turned upside down. Trace around the item with a paring knife.

ITALIAN SLIDER BAKE

PREP TIME: 15 Minutes | **START TO FINISH:** 45 Minutes | 8 sliders

1 can Pillsbury Grands!
Flaky Layers refrigerated
buttermilk biscuits
(8 biscuits)

⅓ cup refrigerated basil pesto
(from 6-oz container)

8 slices deli ham (4 oz)

16 slices deli Genoa salami
(3 oz)

½ cup sliced drained roasted
red bell peppers
(from 12-oz jar)

1 cup finely shredded Italian
cheese blend (4 oz)

1 tablespoon butter, melted

1 tablespoon chopped fresh
basil leaves

1. Heat oven to 400°F. Spray 9-inch square pan with cooking spray. Separate dough into 8 biscuits; place in pan.

2. Bake 9 to 11 minutes or until golden brown. Cool 5 minutes.

3. Remove biscuits from pan by turning upside down onto cutting board. Using sharp serrated knife, cut biscuits in half horizontally. Place bottoms of biscuits cut side up back in pan. Spread cut sides of bottoms with pesto. Arrange ham, salami, roasted peppers and cheese evenly over pesto. Place biscuit tops over cheese.

4. Bake 15 to 20 minutes or until filling is hot and cheese is melted, Cover with foil during last 10 minutes of bake time to prevent over browning if necessary.

5. In small bowl, stir together butter and basil; brush over tops of biscuits. Cut between biscuits before serving. Serve warm.

1 Slider: Calories 340; Total Fat 19g (Saturated Fat 8g, Trans Fat 0g); Cholesterol 35mg; Sodium 1040mg; Total Carbohydrate 28g (Dietary Fiber 0g); Protein 13g **Exchanges:** 1 Starch, 1 Other Carbohydrate, ½ Lean Meat, 1 High-Fat Meat, 2 Fat **Carbohydrate Choices:** 2

KITCHEN SECRET

◆ Genoa salami can be found in the deli of your favorite grocery store.

KITCHEN HACK

COOKED CHICKEN

How do you get cooked chicken for an appetizer without having to cook it first? Purchase rotisserie chicken or frozen cooked chicken from the freezer case. Or cook up a few extra pieces when making chicken for dinner, and freeze up to 9 months until you need it.

CHIPOTLE TURKEY SLIDER BAKE

PREP TIME: 20 Minutes | **START TO FINISH:** 45 Minutes | 8 sliders

1	can Pillsbury Grands! Flaky Layers refrigerated buttermilk biscuits (8 biscuits)
2	tablespoons mayonnaise or salad dressing
1	tablespoon Dijon mustard
1	tablespoon honey
¼ to ½	teaspoon ground chipotle chili pepper
¼	lb thinly sliced cooked deli turkey breast
6	slices Swiss cheese (about 1 oz each)
1	tablespoon chopped fresh parsley
1	tablespoon butter, melted
½	teaspoon poppy seed

1 Heat oven to 400°F. Spray 9-inch square pan with cooking spray. Separate dough into 8 biscuits; place in pan.

2 Bake 10 to 12 minutes or until golden brown. Cool 10 minutes. Reduce oven to 375°F.

3 Meanwhile, in small bowl, stir together mayonnaise, mustard, honey and chili pepper.

4 Remove biscuits from pan by turning upside down onto cutting board. Using sharp serrated knife, cut biscuits in half horizontally. Place bottoms of biscuits cut side up back in pan. Spread half of the mayonnaise mixture evenly over cut sides of biscuits. Arrange turkey and cheese over mayonnaise mixture. Spread remaining mayonnaise mixture over cheese. Place biscuit tops over mayonnaise mixture. In small bowl, stir together parsley, butter and poppy seed; brush over tops of biscuits.

5 Bake 9 to 14 minutes or until cheese is melted and filling is hot. Cut between biscuits before serving. Serve warm.

1 Slider: Calories 320; Total Fat 17g (Saturated Fat 8g, Trans Fat 0g); Cholesterol 30mg; Sodium 740mg; Total Carbohydrate 29g (Dietary Fiber 0g); Protein 12g **Exchanges:** 1 Starch, 1 Other Carbohydrate, 1 Very Lean Meat, ½ High-Fat Meat, 2½ Fat **Carbohydrate Choices:** 2

KITCHEN SECRET

◆ When cutting the sliders apart, be sure to use a serrated knife, and be careful not to cut through to the bottom of the pan.

SERVE IT UP

◆ These appetizers are terrific as is, but you can also serve them as sandwiches with coleslaw and a wedge of watermelon for an easy meal.

CRAB-FILLED CRESCENT WONTONS

PREP TIME: 20 Minutes | **START TO FINISH:** 35 Minutes | **24 wontons**

1 can Pillsbury refrigerated crescent dough sheet

3 oz cream cheese, softened (from 8-oz package)

¾ cup chopped cooked crabmeat

1 tablespoon chopped green onion (1 medium)

⅛ to ¼ teaspoon ground red pepper (cayenne)

1 egg white, beaten

1. Heat oven to 375°F. Spray cookie sheet with cooking spray. Unroll dough on cutting board; cut into 6 rows by 4 rows to make 24 squares.

2. In small bowl, mix cream cheese, crabmeat, onion and red pepper. Spoon about 1 teaspoon crab mixture ½ inch from 1 corner of 1 square. Starting with same corner, fold dough over filling and tuck end tightly underneath filling; continue rolling to within ½ inch of opposite corner. Lightly brush exposed corner with egg white. Roll moistened corner of dough over roll; press to seal. Place on cookie sheet. Brush with egg white. Repeat with remaining squares and filling.

3. Bake 10 to 15 minutes or until golden brown. Remove from cookie sheet. Serve warm.

1 Wonton: Calories 45; Total Fat 2.5g (Saturated Fat 1g, Trans Fat 0g); Cholesterol 10mg; Sodium 105mg; Total Carbohydrate 5g (Dietary Fiber 0g); Protein 1g **Exchanges:** ½ Other Carbohydrate, ½ Fat **Carbohydrate Choices:** ½

KITCHEN SECRETS

◆ Ground red pepper, or cayenne pepper, nicely spices these wontons. Add more if you like.

◆ Cans or foil pouches of crabmeat found near the seafood department are usually of better quality and have better flavor than cans in the canned meat and seafood section. However, either type may be used.

◆ If you prefer, you can use 1 can Pillsbury refrigerated crescent dinner rolls (8 rolls) instead of the dough sheet. Unroll dough and firmly press perforations to seal. Continue as directed.

BEEF STROGANOFF BITES

PREP TIME: 20 Minutes | **START TO FINISH:** 35 Minutes | 24 bites

1   can Pillsbury refrigerated crescent dough sheet

¼   lb lean (at least 80%) ground beef

½   cup finely chopped fresh mushrooms

¼   cup French onion–sour cream dip (from 8-oz container)

3   tablespoons chopped chives

¼   teaspoon pepper

1 Heat oven to 375°F. Spray cookie sheet with cooking spray. Unroll dough on cutting board; cut into 6 rows by 4 rows to make 24 squares.

2 In 10-inch skillet, cook ground beef and mushrooms on medium-high heat until beef is thoroughly cooked; drain well. Stir in sour cream dip, 2 tablespoons of the chives and the pepper.

3 Spoon about 1 teaspoon mixture into center of each square. Bring opposite corners of square over filling; press to seal. Sprinkle with remaining 1 tablespoon chives.

4 Bake 10 to 15 minutes or until golden brown. Immediately remove from cookie sheet. Serve warm.

1 Bite: Calories 40; Total Fat 2g (Saturated Fat 1g, Trans Fat 0g); Cholesterol 0mg; Sodium 95mg; Total Carbohydrate 5g (Dietary Fiber 0g); Protein 1g **Exchanges:** ½ Other Carbohydrate, ½ Fat **Carbohydrate Choices:** ½

KITCHEN SECRET

◆ You can substitute other flavors of sour cream dip if you like.

ADD A GARNISH

◆ Dollop the appetizer bites with sour cream dip and sprinkle with chopped chives before serving.

KITCHEN HACK

DEVILISHLY SMART

Keep deviled eggs from tipping over by cutting a thin slice from the bottom of each hard-cooked egg half before filling the centers.

SAUSAGE–CREAM CHEESE CRESCENT BUNDLES

PREP TIME: 30 Minutes | **START TO FINISH:** 45 Minutes | 24 bundles

½ lb bulk hot pork sausage

1 can Pillsbury refrigerated crescent dough sheet

½ cup spicy jalapeño cream cheese spread (from 8-oz container)

1 Heat oven to 375°F. In 10-inch nonstick skillet, cook sausage over medium-high heat 4 to 5 minutes, stirring frequently, until no longer pink; drain.

2 Unroll dough on cutting board. Starting at center, press into 12x9-inch rectangle. With pizza cutter or sharp knife, cut into 6 rows by 4 rows to make 24 squares.

3 Place about 1 rounded teaspoon sausage in center of each dough square. Top with about 1 teaspoon cream cheese spread. Bring 4 corners together to overlap slightly in center at top of each bundle. Twist and pinch to seal, leaving small gaps between seams. Place on ungreased cookie sheets.

4 Bake 10 to 14 minutes or until golden brown. Serve warm.

1 Bundle: Calories 60; Total Fat 3.5g (Saturated Fat 1.5g, Trans Fat 0g); Cholesterol 10mg; Sodium 135mg; Total Carbohydrate 5g (Dietary Fiber 0g); Protein 2g **Exchanges:** ½ Starch, ½ Fat **Carbohydrate Choices:** ½

KITCHEN SECRETS

◆ Too spicy? Substitute plain cream cheese or garden vegetable cream cheese spread for the spicy jalapeño cream cheese spread.

◆ You can substitute 1 can Pillsbury refrigerated crescent dinner rolls (8 rolls) for the dough sheet if you prefer. Unroll dough and firmly press perforations to seal. Continue as directed.

ADD A GARNISH

◆ Garnish these sausage bites with a dollop of sour cream and a cilantro sprig.

MEXICAN CORN AND BLACK BEAN MINI TURNOVERS

PREP TIME: 35 Minutes | **START TO FINISH:** 55 Minutes | **16 servings**

½ cup frozen (thawed) whole kernel corn

½ cup rinsed drained black beans (from 15-oz can)

1¼ cups prepared salsa verde (from 16-oz jar)

1 cup shredded Mexican cheese blend (4 oz)

1 box Pillsbury refrigerated pie crusts, softened as directed on box

1 egg, beaten

1 medium avocado, pitted, peeled and chopped

2 tablespoons chopped fresh cilantro

1. Heat oven to 400°F. In medium bowl, stir together corn, beans, ¼ cup of the salsa verde and the cheese.

2. On lightly floured work surface, roll each pie crust into 14-inch round. Using 3¼-inch round cutter, cut 14 rounds from each crust, rerolling to make 32 rounds total.

3. Spoon scant tablespoon bean mixture evenly onto one half of each dough round. Brush edge of round with beaten egg. Fold untopped sides of dough rounds over filling; press edges with fork to seal. Place on two ungreased cookie sheets. Brush tops with egg. Cut small slit in top of each turnover for steam to escape.

4. Bake 12 to 16 minutes or until golden brown.

5. Meanwhile, in blender container or bowl of food processor, process remaining 1 cup salsa verde, the avocado and cilantro 5 to 10 seconds or until avocado is finely chopped. Serve salsa with turnovers.

1 Serving (2 Turnovers and 1 Tablespoon Salsa): Calories 160; Total Fat 9g (Saturated Fat 4g, Trans Fat 0g); Cholesterol 25mg; Sodium 280mg; Total Carbohydrate 15g (Dietary Fiber 1g); Protein 3g **Exchanges:** 1 Starch, 1½ Fat **Carbohydrate Choices:** 1

KITCHEN SECRET

◆ For chunkier salsa, mash the avocado with a fork and stir into salsa verde and cilantro.

ADD A GARNISH

◆ Dress up these little turnovers by sprinkling with chopped fresh cilantro and adding a dollop of sour cream, in addition to the salsa.

TUSCAN CRESCENT RING

PREP TIME: 45 Minutes | **START TO FINISH:** 1 Hour 40 Minutes | 8 servings

2   packages (3 oz each) sliced prosciutto, cut into thin strips

1   box (9 oz) frozen chopped spinach, thawed, squeezed to drain

2   containers (7.5 oz each) garden vegetable cream cheese spread

4   oz provolone cheese, shredded (1 cup)

1   teaspoon Italian seasoning

2   cans (8 oz each) Pillsbury refrigerated crescent dough sheet

½   cup chopped seeded tomato

2   tablespoons pine nuts

3   tablespoons shredded Parmesan cheese

KITCHEN SECRETS

◆ For a different twist, substitute 8 slices thickly cut, chopped and crisply cooked bacon for the prosciutto.

◆ If you like, substitute 1 cup finely shredded Italian cheese blend for the provolone cheese.

1   Heat oven to 350°F. Line large cookie sheet with cooking parchment paper.

2   In 10-inch nonstick skillet, cook prosciutto over medium-high heat, stirring occasionally, 6 to 8 minutes or until crisp. Drain on paper towels; set aside.

3   In small bowl, mix spinach, cream cheese, provolone cheese and ½ teaspoon of the Italian seasoning until well blended.

4   Unroll both cans of dough; separate into 16 triangles. On cookie sheet, with shortest sides toward center, arrange triangles in star shape leaving a 6-inch circle in center. Dough will overlap. (Crescent dough points may hang over edge of cookie sheet.) Press overlapping dough to flatten.

5   Sprinkle prosciutto in 2-inch wide strip over half of each triangle closest to center of the ring. Carefully spoon spinach mixture onto prosciutto. Sprinkle with tomatoes and pine nuts.

6   Pull points of triangles up over filling, tucking dough under bottom layer of dough to secure it and form ring. Repeat around ring until entire filling is enclosed (some filling will be visible).

7   In small bowl, stir together Parmesan cheese and remaining ½ teaspoon Italian seasoning; set aside.

8   Bake 25 to 28 minutes or until dough is golden brown and thoroughly baked. Sprinkle with Parmesan mixture. Bake about 8 minutes longer or until cheese is melted. Cool 15 minutes before cutting. Serve warm.

1 Serving: Calories 480; Total Fat 33g (Saturated Fat 17g, Trans Fat 0.5g); Cholesterol 70mg; Sodium 1120mg; Total Carbohydrate 28g (Dietary Fiber 1g); Protein 18g **Exchanges:** 2 Starch, 1 Lean Meat, ½ High-Fat Meat, 5 Fat **Carbohydrate Choices:** 2

CRESCENT DOG PULL-APART WREATH

PREP TIME: 20 Minutes | **START TO FINISH:** 35 Minutes | **15 servings**

1   can Pillsbury refrigerated crescent dough sheet

30   cocktail-size smoked link sausages (from 14-oz package)

1   egg, beaten

1   Heat oven to 375°F. Line large cookie sheet with cooking parchment paper. Unroll dough on cutting board. Starting at center, press into 13x8-inch rectangle. With pizza cutter or sharp knife, cut into 15 squares (about 2½ inches each). Cut each square diagonally in half to make 30 triangles.

2   Place sausage on short side of dough triangle, and roll up. On ungreased cookie sheet, place triangles in circle with sides touching and with every other wrapped sausage extending out slightly. Leave about 6 inches for opening in center of wreath. Brush dough with egg.

3   Bake 12 to 15 minutes or until golden brown. Serve with ketchup, barbecue sauce or honey mustard, if desired.

1 Serving (2 Triangles): Calories 120; Total Fat 8g (Saturated Fat 3g, Trans Fat 0g); Cholesterol 25mg; Sodium 320mg; Total Carbohydrate 8g (Dietary Fiber 0g); Protein 4g **Exchanges:** ½ Other Carbohydrate, ½ Medium-Fat Meat, 1 Fat **Carbohydrate Choices:** ½

KITCHEN SECRETS

◆ If the dough sticks to the work surface, sprinkle with a little flour.

◆ Use the cooking parchment paper to gently lift the baked wreath onto a serving platter. If desired, trim any excess parchment.

ADD A GARNISH

◆ Garnish the wreath with halved grape tomatoes and sprigs of Italian parsley for a colorful presentation.

BBQ MAC-AND-CHEESE APPETIZER PIZZA

PREP TIME: 20 Minutes | **START TO FINISH:** 45 Minutes | **24 servings**

1   can Pillsbury refrigerated classic pizza crust

1½   cups shredded deli rotisserie chicken (from 2-lb chicken)

1   cup barbecue sauce

2   cups prepared macaroni and cheese

½   cup finely shredded Cheddar cheese

1 Heat oven to 400°F. Lightly spray large cookie sheet with cooking spray. Unroll dough on cookie sheet. Starting at center, press into 15x10-inch rectangle.

2 Bake 8 to 10 minutes or until light golden brown.

3 In medium bowl, stir together chicken and ¾ cup of the barbecue sauce. Spoon over crust to within ¼ inch from edges. Spoon macaroni and cheese evenly over chicken. Sprinkle with Cheddar cheese.

4 Bake 8 to 12 minutes or until crust is golden brown and macaroni is hot. Drizzle with remaining ¼ cup barbecue sauce. Cut into 4 rows by 3 rows. Cut each piece diagonally in half.

1 Serving: Calories 120; Total Fat 3.5g (Saturated Fat 1g, Trans Fat 0g); Cholesterol 10mg; Sodium 320mg; Total Carbohydrate 17g (Dietary Fiber 0g); Protein 5g **Exchanges:** ½ Starch, ½ Other Carbohydrate, ½ Lean Meat, ½ Fat **Carbohydrate Choices:** 1

KITCHEN SECRET

◆ If you don't have prepared macaroni and cheese, you can purchase refrigerated, frozen or boxed macaroni and cheese and prepare as directed.

ADD A GARNISH

◆ After drizzling baked pizza with barbecue sauce, sprinkle with thinly sliced green onion for an easy garnish.

MARGHERITA PIZZA BREAD

PREP TIME: 15 Minutes | **START TO FINISH:** 1 Hour | **12 slices**

1   can Pillsbury refrigerated
     classic pizza crust

¾   cup chopped
     seeded tomatoes

1   cup shredded mozzarella
     cheese (4 oz)

1   tablespoon chopped fresh
     basil leaves or 1 teaspoon
     dried basil leaves

2   teaspoons pizza seasoning

1   egg yolk

1   tablespoon water

1   Heat oven to 375°F. Spray cookie sheet with cooking spray. Unroll dough on cookie sheet. Starting at center, press into 14x11-inch rectangle.

2   Pat tomatoes with paper towels to dry. In medium bowl, combine tomatoes, cheese, basil and 1½ teaspoons of the pizza seasoning. Sprinkle over crust. Starting at a long edge; roll up. Press seam to seal. Place seam side down on cookie sheet. Turn ends under to seal.

3   In small bowl, mix egg yolk and water with fork until well blended. Brush over dough; sprinkle with remaining ½ teaspoon pizza seasoning.

4   Bake 25 to 27 minutes or until golden brown. Cool 10 minutes. Cut into 1-inch slices. Serve warm.

1 Slice: Calories 120; Total Fat 3.5g (Saturated Fat 1.5g, Trans Fat 0g); Cholesterol 20mg; Sodium 250mg; Total Carbohydrate 17g (Dietary Fiber 0g); Protein 5g **Exchanges:** 1 Starch, ½ Fat **Carbohydrate Choices:** 1

KITCHEN SECRETS

◆ If you don't have pizza seasoning, substitute 2 teaspoons Italian seasoning.

◆ Seeding the tomatoes and patting them dry removes most of the liquid so the bread won't become gummy.

MEDITERRANEAN HUMMUS SALAD FLATBREAD

PREP TIME: 20 Minutes | **START TO FINISH:** 55 Minutes | **32 servings**

1 can Pillsbury refrigerated crescent dough sheet or 1 can Pillsbury refrigerated crescent dinner rolls (8 rolls)

1 cup prepared hummus

1 cup fresh arugula leaves

⅔ cup grape tomatoes, cut in half

⅓ cup thin slices cucumber, cut in half

½ cup crumbled feta cheese

¼ cup Italian dressing

1 Heat oven to 375°F. Spray large cookie sheet with cooking spray. Unroll dough onto cookie sheet; press into 13x9-inch rectangle. If using crescent rolls, firmly press perforations to seal.

2 Bake 9 to 11 minutes or until golden brown. Cool completely, about 20 minutes.

3 Spread hummus over crust, to within ½-inch of edges. Top with arugula, tomatoes, cucumber and feta cheese. Drizzle with dressing. Serve immediately, or cover and refrigerate up to 2 hours before serving. Cut into 8 rows by 4 rows.

1 Serving: Calories 50; Total Fat 2.5g (Saturated Fat 1g, Trans Fat 0g); Cholesterol 0mg; Sodium 130mg; Total Carbohydrate 5g (Dietary Fiber 0g); Protein 1g **Exchanges:** ½ Starch, ½ Fat **Carbohydrate Choices:** ½

KITCHEN SECRETS

◆ If you like olives, go ahead and add them to the top of this pizza!

◆ Fresh baby spinach leaves can be used in place of the arugula leaves.

SERVE IT UP

◆ Bring something new to the party! This flatbread can be served as an appetizer, snack or light meal.

PROVENÇAL FLATBREAD

PREP TIME: 30 Minutes | **START TO FINISH:** 30 Minutes | **24 servings**

1 can Pillsbury refrigerated classic pizza crust

3 tablespoons extra-virgin olive oil

1 teaspoon herbes de Provence

3 plum (Roma) tomatoes, finely chopped (¾ cup)

½ cup chopped pitted kalamata olives

2 teaspoons chopped fresh basil leaves

1 teaspoon freshly ground pepper

½ teaspoon coarse sea salt

4 cloves garlic, chopped

1 Heat oven to 400°F. Spray large cookie sheet with cooking spray. Unroll dough on cookie sheet. Starting at center, press dough into 15x10-inch rectangle. Brush with 1 tablespoon of the oil; sprinkle with herbes de Provence.

2 Bake 15 to 18 minutes or until light golden brown.

3 Meanwhile, in medium bowl, mix tomatoes, olives, remaining 2 tablespoons oil, the chopped basil, pepper, salt and garlic.

4 Cut flatbread into 6 rows by 4 rows. Top evenly with tomato mixture.

1 Serving: Calories 80; Total Fat 4.5g (Saturated Fat 0.5g, Trans Fat 0g); Cholesterol 0mg; Sodium 288mg; Total Carbohydrate 9g (Dietary Fiber 0.5g); Protein 1.5g **Exchanges:** ½ Starch, ½ Fat **Carbohydrate Choices:** ½

KITCHEN SECRET

◆ Herbes de Provence is a blend of herbs that thrive in the southeastern tip of France, typically thyme, summer savory, fennel, basil and lavender flowers. It is readily available in larger grocery stores, in cooking supply stores or online.

ADD A GARNISH

◆ Garnish this flatbread with fresh basil leaves or rosemary sprigs.

CRESCENT DOUGH SHEET HACKS

With these great ideas, you'll have oodles of options to impress and satisfy!

APPETIZER OR DESSERT CUPS
(bottom left)

Cut dough into 6 rows by 4 rows. Place 1 square into each of 24 mini muffin cups. Bake and fill.

BREAKFAST PIZZAS *(bottom right)*

Cut dough into 4 rectangles. Top with favorite breakfast ingredients; bake.

CINNAMON CRESCENT ROLLS
(upper left)

Spread dough with a little softened butter; sprinkle with cinnamon-sugar and chopped nuts. Roll up and bake. Drizzle warm rolls with favorite glaze.

PINWHEELS *(upper right)*

Spread dough with desired fillings. Roll up, slice and bake.

WONTONS *(bottom left)*

Cut dough into 6 rows by 4 rows. Spoon 1 teaspoon filling onto each dough square. Bring two opposite corners up over filling; press and bake.

SWEET BREADS

APPLE-FILLED CINNAMON-SUGAR DOUGHNUTS

PREP TIME: 20 Minutes | **START TO FINISH:** 40 Minutes | 8 doughnuts

1 can Pillsbury Grands!™ Flaky Layers Original refrigerated biscuits (8 biscuits)

1 small Granny Smith apple, peeled, cored

⅓ cup sugar

1 teaspoon ground cinnamon

2 tablespoons butter, melted

1 Heat oven to 350°F. Spray cookie sheet with cooking spray.

2 Separate dough into 8 biscuits. Press or roll each into 5-inch round. Cut apple into 8 (¼ inch) rings. Place 1 apple ring in center of each round. In small bowl, mix sugar and cinnamon. Sprinkle about 1 teaspoon cinnamon-sugar over each apple ring.

3 Wrap biscuit around each apple ring to cover completely, pinching ends together to form tight seal. Place biscuits sealed side down on cookie sheet.

4 Bake 18 to 22 minutes or until biscuits are deep golden brown. Brush tops of biscuits with melted butter and sprinkle with remaining cinnamon-sugar. Serve immediately.

1 Doughnut: Calories 250; Total Fat 9g (Saturated Fat 4.5g, Trans Fat 0g); Cholesterol 10mg; Sodium 470mg; Total Carbohydrate 37g (Dietary Fiber 1g); Protein 4g **Exchanges:** 1½ Starch, 1 Other Carbohydrate, 1½ Fat **Carbohydrate Choices:** 2½

KITCHEN SECRETS

◆ These doughnuts taste best straight out of the oven. To make up to 2 hours ahead, prepare as directed through step 3, then cover and refrigerate until ready to bake. When ready, uncover and bake as directed.

◆ Sprinkle with powdered sugar instead of the cinnamon-sugar for a fun variation.

ADD A GARNISH

◆ Drizzle doughnuts with caramel sauce for a pretty presentation.

COCONUT-ALMOND POP-EMS

PREP TIME: 35 Minutes | **START TO FINISH:** 50 Minutes | 32 pop-ems

1 can Pillsbury Grands! Flaky Layers Original refrigerated biscuits (8 biscuits)

¾ cup whole almonds

1½ cups shredded coconut

2 cups powdered sugar

3 tablespoons milk

2 teaspoons vanilla

½ teaspoon almond extract

1. Heat oven to 350°F. Separate dough into 8 biscuits; cut each into 4 pieces. Roll each piece firmly, shaping into a ball. Place 1 inch apart on ungreased cookie sheet.

2. Bake 13 to 17 minutes or until light golden brown. Remove to cooling rack; cool 5 minutes.

3. Meanwhile, in food processor, place almonds. Process 15 to 30 seconds until almonds are ground. Transfer almonds to shallow dish. Place coconut in another shallow dish. In small bowl, combine powdered sugar, milk, vanilla and almond extract; beat with whisk until blended and smooth.

4. Line cookie sheet with cooking parchment paper. When cooled, dip half of each pop-em into glaze, allowing excess glaze to drip off before dipping glazed portion into almonds. Place on parchment-lined cookie sheet.

5. Dip the uncoated side of each pop-em into glaze, allowing excess glaze to drip off before dipping into coconut. Place on cookie sheet. Let stand 5 minutes for glaze to set. Store tightly covered.

1 Pop-em: Calories 120; Total Fat 4.5g (Saturated Fat 2g, Trans Fat 0g); Cholesterol 0mg; Sodium 125mg; Total Carbohydrate 17g (Dietary Fiber 0g); Protein 2g **Exchanges:** 1 Starch, 1 Fat **Carbohydrate Choices:** 1

KITCHEN HACK

SOFTEN BUTTER

Let stick of butter stand at room temperature about 30 minutes. Or for faster softening, remove wrapper and place butter in microwavable bowl; microwave on Low (30%) 20 to 40 seconds.

GERMAN CHOCOLATE—COCONUT BAKED DOUGHNUTS

PREP TIME: 20 Minutes | START TO FINISH: 35 Minutes | 8 doughnuts

1   can Pillsbury Grands! Flaky Layers refrigerated buttermilk biscuits (8 biscuits)

1   cup coconut

1   cup coconut-pecan creamy ready-to-spread frosting (from 14.5-oz container)

¼   cup chopped pecans

⅓   cup hot fudge topping

1   Heat oven to 375°F. Separate dough into 8 biscuits. With 1-inch round cookie cutter, cut hole in center of each biscuit. Place coconut in shallow dish. Dip both sides of biscuits and holes into coconut; press lightly. Place on ungreased large cookie sheet about 2 inches apart.

2   Bake 10 to 15 minutes or until golden brown. Remove from cookie sheet to cooling rack; cool 2 minutes. Frost doughnuts with frosting; sprinkle with pecans. Heat hot fudge topping as directed on jar; drizzle over doughnuts.

1 Doughnut: Calories 440; Total Fat 20g (Saturated Fat 9g, Trans Fat 1g); Cholesterol 0mg; Sodium 580mg; Total Carbohydrate 59g (Dietary Fiber 2g); Protein 5g **Exchanges:** 1 Starch, 3 Other Carbohydrate, ½ High-Fat Meat, 3 Fat **Carbohydrate Choices:** 4

KITCHEN SECRET

◆ Pecans are traditional for German chocolate cake or, in this case, doughnuts, but you can use chopped walnuts or almonds as well.

SERVE IT UP

◆ Serve these easy doughnuts at a brunch or a breakfast buffet where you can have warm doughnuts in minutes. Serve alongside scrambled eggs with cheese and cooked veggies stirred in at the end.

KITCHEN HACK

BAKE RIGHT

Over time, ovens lose their ability to maintain the correct temperature. Use an oven thermometer to ensure that your oven is at the correct temperature. Adjust the heat setting if needed.

CINNAMON ROLL BUNNIES

PREP TIME: 15 Minutes | **START TO FINISH:** 45 Minutes | 4 bunnies

1 can Pillsbury Flaky refrigerated cinnamon rolls with butter cream icing (8 rolls)

8 semisweet chocolate chips

4 red baking chips or candy-coated chocolate candies

8 almond slices

1 Heat oven to 350°F. Spray cookie sheet with cooking spray.

2 Separate dough into 8 rolls. Place 4 of the rolls on cookie sheet about 3 inches apart. Unwind remaining 4 rolls into long dough strips. For each bunny, place 1 dough strip, cut ends together, next to a whole roll. Press and firmly pinch cut ends into top of whole roll. Shape strip into floppy bunny ears.

3 On each bunny, place 2 chocolate chips for eyes, 1 red baking chip for nose and 2 almond slices for teeth; press firmly into dough.

4 Bake 12 to 15 minutes or until golden brown. Cool 5 minutes; remove from cookie sheet to cooling rack. Spread icing on warm rolls. Serve warm.

1 Bunny: Calories 340; Total Fat 15g (Saturated Fat 6g, Trans Fat 0g); Cholesterol 0mg; Sodium 660mg; Total Carbohydrate 47g (Dietary Fiber 1g); Protein 4g **Exchanges:** 1½ Starch, 1½ Other Carbohydrate, 3 Fat **Carbohydrate Choices:** 3

KITCHEN SECRET

◆ Make each bunny unique by shaping the ears a bit differently for each one.

KITCHEN HACK

SOFT BROWN SUGAR

Store the heal from a loaf of bread with the brown sugar to keep the brown sugar from getting hard.

PEANUT BUTTER–BANANA ROLLS

PREP TIME: 25 Minutes | **START TO FINISH:** 50 Minutes | 12 rolls

ROLLS

⅓ cup powdered sugar

¼ cup creamy peanut butter

2 tablespoons butter, softened

½ teaspoon banana extract

2 cans Pillsbury refrigerated original breadsticks (12 breadsticks each)

GLAZE

½ cup milk chocolate baking chips

3 tablespoons butter

2 teaspoons light corn syrup

⅛ teaspoon vanilla

⅛ teaspoon banana extract

TOPPING

¼ cup chopped pecans

1 Heat oven to 375°F. Spray large cookie sheet with cooking spray. In small bowl, stir powdered sugar, peanut butter, 2 tablespoons butter and ½ teaspoon banana extract until smooth; set aside.

2 Unroll both cans of dough on cutting board; divide each into 4 equal sections along center perforations. Spread about ¼ cup peanut butter mixture over each of 2 dough sections. Place remaining 2 dough sections over filling. Using sharp knife, cut along perforations into 12 strips. Gently stretch each strip until about 10 inches long. Twist each strip 4 or 5 times. Coil each strip into pinwheel shape; tuck end under. Place 2 inches apart on cookie sheet.

3 Bake 12 to 18 minutes or until golden brown. Remove rolls from cookie sheet to cooling rack placed on waxed paper. Cool 10 minutes.

4 Meanwhile, in 2-quart saucepan, melt chocolate chips, 3 tablespoons butter and the corn syrup over medium heat, stirring occasionally, until chocolate chips are melted and mixture is smooth. Stir in vanilla and ⅛ teaspoon banana extract.

5 Drizzle glaze over warm rolls. Sprinkle each roll with 1 teaspoon pecans. Serve warm or at room temperature.

1 Roll: Calories 290; Total Fat 13g (Saturated Fat 5g, Trans Fat 0g); Cholesterol 15mg; Sodium 350mg; Total Carbohydrate 36g (Dietary Fiber 0g); Protein 6g **Exchanges:** 1 Starch, 1½ Other Carbohydrate, ½ High-Fat Meat, 1½ Fat **Carbohydrate Choices:** 2½

KITCHEN SECRET

◆ Banana extract provides a subtle banana flavor to these rolls. You can find it next to the vanilla extract in the spice aisle of your grocery store.

HONEY-ORANGE BLOSSOMS

PREP TIME: 15 Minutes | **START TO FINISH:** 45 Minutes | 8 rolls

1 can Pillsbury refrigerated cinnamon rolls with cream cheese icing (8 rolls)

1/3 cup honey-nut cream cheese spread (from 8-oz container)

2 tablespoons finely chopped walnuts

1 teaspoon grated orange peel

1 Heat oven to 350°F. Spray 8 regular-size muffin cups with cooking spray. Set icing from cinnamon rolls aside. Separate dough into 8 rolls; cut each roll into 4 pieces. In each muffin cup, place 4 pieces, with points up and cinnamon topping facing in, and slightly separated.

2 In small bowl, mix cream cheese spread, walnuts and ½ teaspoon of the orange peel. Spoon 1 rounded teaspoonful of mixture into center of dough in each cup.

3 Bake 17 to 22 minutes or until light golden brown. Cool 5 minutes. Run knife around edge of cups; remove rolls from cups to serving plate.

4 Remove cover from reserved icing. Microwave on Medium (50%) 5 to 10 seconds or until thin enough to drizzle. Stir in remaining ½ teaspoon orange peel. Drizzle icing over rolls. Serve warm.

1 Roll: Calories 200; Total Fat 10g (Saturated Fat 3.5g, Trans Fat 0g); Cholesterol 0mg; Sodium 390mg; Total Carbohydrate 25g (Dietary Fiber 0g); Protein 3g **Exchanges:** 1 Starch, 1 Other Carbohydrate, 1½ Fat **Carbohydrate Choices:** 1½

KITCHEN SECRET

◆ Feel free to swap out the finely chopped walnuts for another nut.

SERVE IT UP

◆ Serve these with scrambled, fried or your favorite type of eggs, and watch the smiles come to life!

KITCHEN HACK

WAFFLES ON DEMAND

Extra waffles or pancakes can be kept on hand for quick weekday breakfasts. Cool them on a cooling rack and store in resealable freezer plastic bags. To reheat waffles, place in toaster until hot. For pancakes, place 3 pancakes on microwavable plate and microwave 1 minute or until hot.

BREAKFAST BAKLAVA

PREP TIME: 35 Minutes | **START TO FINISH:** 1 Hour | **8 servings**

SYRUP

- ½ cup honey
- ⅓ cup water
- ¼ cup sugar
- 2 teaspoons lemon juice
- ⅛ teaspoon ground cinnamon
  Dash salt
- 3 whole cloves or dash ground cloves

FILLING

- ½ cup sliced blanched almonds
- ¼ cup walnut halves and pieces
- 1 tablespoon sugar
- ½ teaspoon ground cinnamon
  Dash salt, if desired

BISCUITS

- 1 can Pillsbury Grands! Flaky Layers Butter Tastin'™ refrigerated biscuits (8 biscuits)

1. Heat oven to 350°F. Generously spray 8 regular-size nonstick muffin cups with cooking spray.

2. In 1-quart saucepan, mix syrup ingredients; heat to boiling. Remove from heat; cool 10 minutes. Discard whole cloves.

3. Meanwhile, in food processor bowl with metal blade, place filling ingredients. Cover; process with on-and-off pulses until finely chopped. Set aside.

4. Separate dough into 8 biscuits; separate each biscuit into 3 layers. Place 1 biscuit layer in bottom of each muffin cup. For each biscuit layer, brush dough with syrup; top with 1½ teaspoons filling and drizzle with 1½ teaspoons syrup. Place second biscuit layer on top; press edge of second biscuit into side of bottom biscuit. Brush with syrup; top with 1½ teaspoons filling and drizzle with 1½ teaspoons syrup. Top with third biscuit layer. Brush with syrup; sprinkle with 1 teaspoon filling. Repeat with remaining biscuits, filling and syrup. Reserve remaining syrup (about ½ cup).

5. Bake 18 to 22 minutes or until deep golden brown. Cool 1 minute. Remove from pan. Serve warm with remaining syrup.

1 Serving: Calories 340; Total Fat 11g (Saturated Fat 3g, Trans Fat 0g); Cholesterol 0mg; Sodium 490mg; Total Carbohydrate 53g (Dietary Fiber 1g); Protein 6g **Exchanges:** 1 Starch, 2½ Other Carbohydrate, ½ High-Fat Meat, 1½ Fat **Carbohydrate Choices:** 3½

KITCHEN SECRET

◆ To make ahead, prepare as directed through step 4; cover and refrigerate overnight. Bake as directed. Reheat reserved ½ cup syrup in microwave on High 30 to 60 seconds until hot.

Clockwise from top:
French Toast Waffles with
Apple-Cherry Topping
(page 78)
Quick and Fruity Crescent
Waffles (right)
Chocolate Chip–Peanut
Butter Waffles (page 79)

QUICK AND FRUITY CRESCENT WAFFLES

PREP TIME: 25 Minutes | START TO FINISH: 25 Minutes | 4 servings

¼ cup pecan pieces

1 can Pillsbury refrigerated crescent dinner rolls (8 rolls)

½ cup blueberry spreadable fruit

1 container (6 oz) blueberry yogurt

1 firm ripe banana, cut into ¼ inch slices

½ cup whipped cream from aerosol can

¼ teaspoon ground cinnamon

1 Heat square or rectangular waffle maker according to manufacturer's directions. Spray with cooking spray.

2 Meanwhile, in 8-inch nonstick skillet, toast pecans over medium heat 5 to 7 minutes, stirring frequently, until lightly browned. Remove from skillet; set aside.

3 Separate crescent dough into 8 triangles. Place 2 or 3 triangles at a time on hot waffle maker, leaving at least ½ inch of space around each triangle. Close lid of waffle maker; bake 1 to 2 minutes or until golden brown.

4 In 1-quart saucepan, heat spreadable fruit and yogurt over medium heat 2 to 3 minutes, stirring occasionally, until hot.

5 Stack 2 crescent waffles, slightly overlapping, on each of 4 serving plates. For each serving, spoon one-fourth of the fruit sauce over waffles. Top with one-fourth of the banana slices and 1 tablespoon of the pecans. Top with whipped cream; sprinkle lightly with cinnamon.

1 Serving (2 Waffles): Calories 480; Total Fat 17g (Saturated Fat 6g, Trans Fat 0g); Cholesterol 10mg; Sodium 440mg; Total Carbohydrate 76g (Dietary Fiber 1g); Protein 6g **Exchanges:** 2 Starch, 3 Other Carbohydrate, 3 Fat **Carbohydrate Choices:** 5

KITCHEN SECRET

◆ To keep waffles warm until serving time, place them in a single layer on a wire rack or paper towel–lined cookie sheet in a 350°F oven up to 20 minutes. Just make sure you don't stack warm waffles because they will become soggy.

ADD A GARNISH

◆ Garnish with fresh blueberries or any berry you prefer.

FRENCH TOAST WAFFLES WITH APPLE-CHERRY TOPPING

PREP TIME: 20 Minutes | **START TO FINISH:** 20 Minutes | 4 servings

1	can (21 oz) apple pie filling
¼	cup cherry preserves
2	eggs
½	cup heavy whipping cream
1½	teaspoons ground cinnamon
1	can Pillsbury Place 'N Bake™ refrigerated crescent rounds (8 rounds)
1½	teaspoons brown sugar

1. Heat waffle maker according to manufacturer's directions. In 1½-quart saucepan, mix apple pie filling and cherry preserves. Cook over low heat, stirring frequently, until warm. Remove from heat; cover to keep warm.

2. In shallow dish, beat eggs, 1 tablespoon of the whipping cream and 1 teaspoon of the cinnamon with whisk until foamy. Separate dough into 8 rounds. Dip each round into egg mixture, coating well. Place 2 to 4 rounds in waffle maker; close lid of waffle maker. Bake 3 to 4 minutes or until crisp and golden brown. Repeat with remaining rounds.

3. Meanwhile, in medium bowl, beat remaining whipping cream, remaining ½ teaspoon cinnamon and the brown sugar with electric mixer on high speed until stiff peaks form.

4. Spoon warm apple mixture over waffles; top with whipped cream.

1 Serving (2 Waffles): Calories 590; Total Fat 24g (Saturated Fat 12g, Trans Fat 0g); Cholesterol 125mg; Sodium 470mg; Total Carbohydrate 84g (Dietary Fiber 2g); Protein 9g **Exchanges:** 2 Starch, 3½ Other Carbohydrate, ½ Medium-Fat Meat, 4 Fat **Carbohydrate Choices:** 5½

KITCHEN SECRET

◆ If you can't find the dough rounds, use 1 can Pillsbury refrigerated crescent dough sheet. Unroll dough on cutting board. Cut into 4 rectangles; press each into 8x4-inch rectangle. Cut each in half crosswise to make 8 squares. Dip each square into egg mixture, coating well. Place 2 to 4 squares in waffle maker; close lid of waffle maker. Continue as directed.

KITCHEN HACK

EASY SLIDE

Spray a liquid measuring cup or measuring spoon with cooking spray before adding thick liquids like honey or syrup so they will pour out easily and not stick to the measuring vessel.

CHOCOLATE CHIP–PEANUT BUTTER WAFFLES

PREP TIME: 30 Minutes | **START TO FINISH:** 30 Minutes | 4 servings

1   roll (16.5 oz) Pillsbury refrigerated chocolate chip cookies

⅓   cup milk

¼   cup creamy peanut butter

2   eggs

2   ripe bananas, sliced

3   tablespoons honey

1   Heat waffle maker to medium-low heat. (Waffle maker without a nonstick coating may need to be brushed with oil or sprayed with cooking spray before batter for each waffle is added.) Let cookie dough stand at room temperature 10 minutes to soften.

2   In large bowl, break up cookie dough. Add milk, peanut butter and eggs. Beat with electric mixer on medium speed 1 to 2 minutes, scraping bowl as needed, until well blended.

3   Pour ⅓ to ½ cup batter onto center of each waffle section of hot waffle maker. (Check manufacturer's directions for recommended amount of batter.) Close lid of waffle maker; bake about 3 minutes or until golden brown.

4   Top each waffle with sliced bananas; drizzle with honey.

1 Serving (2 Waffles): Calories 780; Total Fat 35g (Saturated Fat 13g, Trans Fat 0g); Cholesterol 105mg; Sodium 480mg; Total Carbohydrate 103g (Dietary Fiber 2g); Protein 12g **Exchanges:** 1½ Starch, 5½ Other Carbohydrate, 1 Medium-Fat Meat, 6 Fat **Carbohydrate Choices:** 7

KITCHEN SECRETS

◆ To keep waffles warm until serving time, place them in single layer on a wire rack or paper towel–lined cookie sheet in a 350°F oven up to 20 minutes. Just make sure you don't stack warm waffles, because they will become soggy.

◆ Waffles can be frozen and thawed for later use. Just pop them in the toaster for a quick morning bite.

EASY MINI MONKEY BREADS

PREP TIME: 5 Minutes | START TO FINISH: 20 Minutes | 8 monkey breads

1 can Pillsbury refrigerated cinnamon rolls with cream cheese icing (8 rolls)

1 Heat oven to 400°F. Spray 8 regular-size muffin cups with cooking spray. Set icing aside.

2 Separate dough into 8 rolls. Cut each roll into 6 pieces; place 6 pieces in each muffin cup.

3 Bake 10 minutes. Cool 2 minutes; remove to serving tray.

4 Meanwhile, transfer icing to small microwavable measuring cup. Microwave uncovered on High 6 to 8 seconds or until melted. Drizzle over monkey breads.

1 Monkey Bread: Calories 140; Total Fat 4.5g (Saturated Fat 2.5g, Trans Fat 0g); Cholesterol 0mg; Sodium 350mg; Total Carbohydrate 23g (Dietary Fiber 0g); Protein 2g **Exchanges:** ½ Starch, 1 Other Carbohydrate, 1 Fat **Carbohydrate Choices:** 1½

KITCHEN SECRETS

◆ For a cute presentation, stack the mini monkey breads in a pyramid, and drizzle the icing over the whole stack.

◆ For extra flair, stir a few drops of food color into the icing before drizzling.

KITCHEN HACK

DELICIOUS DOUGHNUTS

Keep doughnuts from getting greasy by making sure the oil is at the temperature called for in the recipe when you drop the doughnuts into it. Drain cooked doughnuts on paper towel–lined cooling racks.

APPLE–CREAM CHEESE MONKEY BREADS

PREP TIME: 30 Minutes | **START TO FINISH:** 55 Minutes | **8 monkey breads**

¼ cup sugar

1 teaspoon ground cinnamon

1 package (8 oz) cream cheese, softened

1½ teaspoons milk

1 can Pillsbury refrigerated crescent dinner rolls (8 rolls)

¾ cup canned apple pie filling, chopped

1. Heat oven to 375°F. Spray 8 regular-size muffin cups with cooking spray.

2. In small bowl, mix 3 tablespoons of the sugar and the cinnamon; set aside. In another small bowl, mix cream cheese, remaining 1 tablespoon sugar and the milk until smooth.

3. Unroll dough on work surface; press perforations to seal. Cut into 8 squares. Cut each square into 5 rows by 4 rows to make 20 mini squares each: Place 20 squares in bottoms and halfway up sides of muffin cups.

4. For each bread, sprinkle ½ teaspoon cinnamon-sugar over top of dough. Spoon about 2 teaspoons cream cheese mixture over cinnamon-sugar and 1 rounded tablespoon pie filling over cream cheese mixture. Sprinkle with another ½ teaspoon cinnamon-sugar.

5. Bake 16 to 20 minutes or until golden brown. Cool 5 minutes. Run small spatula or knife around edge of cups; remove breads from cups to serving plate. Serve warm.

1 Monkey Bread: Calories 190; Total Fat 9g (Saturated Fat 4g, Trans Fat 0g); Cholesterol 10mg; Sodium 250mg; Total Carbohydrate 26g (Dietary Fiber 0g); Protein 2g **Exchanges:** 1 Starch, ½ Other Carbohydrate, 1½ Fat **Carbohydrate Choices:** 2

KITCHEN SECRETS

◆ To chop the apple pie filling, measure the filling, spoon it onto the cutting board, and chop the apple slices using a sharp knife.

◆ For easier cutting, use a pizza cutter to cut dough into strips and squares.

PEANUT BUTTER-CARAMEL STICKY ROLLS

PREP TIME: 20 Minutes | **START TO FINISH:** 55 Minutes | **12 rolls**

½ cup powdered sugar

½ cup caramel topping

¼ cup creamy peanut butter

2 cans (8 oz each) Pillsbury refrigerated crescent dough sheet

½ cup chocolate-flavored hazelnut spread

1. Heat oven to 400°F. Place paper or foil baking cup in each of 12 regular-size muffin cups. Generously spray with cooking spray.

2. In small bowl, mix powdered sugar, caramel topping and peanut butter until blended. Unroll both cans of dough on cutting boards. Spread half of the caramel mixture evenly over each dough sheet to within ½ inch of edges. Starting on short side, roll up each dough sheet. Cut each roll crosswise into 6 pieces; place pieces cut sides up in muffin cup.

3. Bake 12 to 18 minutes or until golden brown. Remove from pan to cooling rack. Cool 15 minutes.

4. Meanwhile, in small microwavable bowl, microwave hazelnut spread on High 30 to 60 seconds. Drizzle over rolls.

1 Roll: Calories 290; Total Fat 13g (Saturated Fat 4g, Trans Fat 0g); Cholesterol 0mg; Sodium 390mg; Total Carbohydrate 38g (Dietary Fiber 0g); Protein 4g **Exchanges:** 2½ Other Carbohydrate, ½ High-Fat Meat, 2 Fat **Carbohydrate Choices:** 2½

SERVE IT UP

◆ These decadent rolls are great as an easy breakfast treat. Pair them with sliced cheese and fresh fruit for a no-fuss breakfast.

KITCHEN HACK

SMART ORDER

If you need both lemon zest and lemon juice, first zest the lemon and then cut it in half and squeeze out the lemon juice.

MAPLE-CASHEW CINNAMON TWISTS

PREP TIME: 10 Minutes | **START TO FINISH:** 30 Minutes | **8 twists**

1 Pillsbury refrigerated pie crust, softened as directed on box

2 tablespoons cinnamon-sugar

¼ cup plus tablespoons chopped cashews

¼ cup powdered sugar

2 tablespoons maple-flavored syrup

1. Heat oven to 425°F. Spray large cookie sheet with cooking spray. Using hands or rolling pin, shape pie crust into 11-inch square.

2. Sprinkle half of dough with cinnamon-sugar. Sprinkle with ¼ cup of the cashews; press gently. Fold pastry in half; cut crosswise into 8 strips. Twist each strip two or three times; place 1 inch apart on cookie sheet.

3. Bake 8 to 10 minutes or until golden brown. Remove twists from pan to cooling rack. Cool 10 minutes.

4. Meanwhile, in small bowl, mix powdered sugar and syrup until smooth. Spread on top of warm twists; sprinkle with remaining cashews.

1 Twist: Calories 180; Total Fat 9g (Saturated Fat 3g, Trans Fat 0g); Cholesterol 5mg; Sodium 135mg; Total Carbohydrate 24g (Dietary Fiber 0g); Protein 1g **Exchanges:** 1½ Other Carbohydrate, 2 Fat **Carbohydrate Choices:** 1½

KITCHEN SECRETS

◆ It's easy to make a double batch of these sweet maple sticks to serve for brunch or a holiday meal. Be sure to use two large cookie sheets and bake separately.

◆ You can make your own cinnamon-sugar mixture with 2 tablespoons granulated sugar and 1 teaspoon ground cinnamon.

Clockwise from top left:
Maple-Cashew Cinnamon
Twists (above)
Apple-Spice Crescent
Twist Loaf (page 88)
Chai-Coconut Twist
Muffins (page 89)

KITCHEN HACK

GET IT ALL

Get every bit of sticky liquids out of the measuring cup or spoon by using a small, flexible rubber scraper to scrape it out with ease.

APPLE-SPICE CRESCENT TWIST LOAF

PREP TIME: 30 Minutes | **START TO FINISH:** 2 Hours 5 Minutes | 10 slices

2 tablespoons butter

2 cups chopped peeled baking apples (about 2 medium)

3 tablespoons packed brown sugar

½ teaspoon apple pie spice

2 tablespoons real maple or maple-flavored syrup

2 cans (8 oz each) Pillsbury refrigerated crescent dough sheet

2 tablespoons finely chopped walnuts

KITCHEN SECRETS

◆ If you don't have apple pie spice, use 1½ teaspoons ground cinnamon and ½ teaspoon ground nutmeg instead.

◆ Use baking apples such as Braeburn, Granny Smith or Gala.

1 Heat oven to 375°F. Line 8x4-inch or 9x5-inch loaf pan with cooking parchment paper, or spray with cooking spray.

2 In 10-inch nonstick skillet, melt butter over medium-high heat. Add apples, brown sugar, apple pie spice and 1 tablespoon of the syrup. Cook over medium heat, stirring occasionally, 5 to 8 minutes or until sugar is dissolved and liquid is consistency of thick syrup. Remove from heat. Cool 5 minutes.

3 Meanwhile, unroll one dough sheet on cutting board. Starting at center, press or roll into 15x9-inch rectangle. Spoon apple mixture evenly over dough sheet to within ¼ inch of edges.

4 Place remaining dough sheet on top of apple-topped dough sheet, stretching slightly to fit. Starting at one long side, roll dough up; pinch seam to seal. Place seam side down on cutting board.

5 Using sharp serrated knife, slice dough lengthwise to within ½ inch from bottom of dough. Keeping cut side up, bring ends together to form U shape with sides touching. Gently twist dough together; place in loaf pan.

6 Bake 40 to 45 minutes or until deep golden brown and loaf is no longer doughy in center. Loosely cover with foil during last 15 minutes of bake time to prevent over browning. Remove foil; place loaf pan on cooling rack. Cool 10 minutes; remove loaf from pan to cooling rack.

7 Brush with remaining syrup; sprinkle with walnuts. Cool 30 minutes. Carefully slice loaf using serrated knife. Serve warm.

1 Slice: Calories 210; Total Fat 8g (Saturated Fat 3.5g, Trans Fat 0g); Cholesterol 5mg; Sodium 380mg; Total Carbohydrate 32g (Dietary Fiber 0g); Protein 2g **Exchanges:** 1 Starch, 1 Other Carbohydrate, 1½ Fat **Carbohydrate Choices:** 2

CHAI-COCONUT TWIST MUFFINS

PREP TIME: 15 Minutes | **START TO FINISH:** 40 Minutes | **8 muffins**

TWISTS

2　cans (8 oz each) Pillsbury refrigerated crescent dough sheet

2　tablespoons butter, softened

2　tablespoons granulated sugar

1　tablespoon chai spice seasoning

½　cup coconut

GLAZE

¾　cup powdered sugar

2 to 3　teaspoons milk

1 Heat oven to 375°F. Spray 8 regular-size muffin cups with cooking spray.

2 Unroll 1 can of the dough on cutting board. Starting at center, press into 12x8-inch rectangle. Spread butter evenly over dough to within ¼ inch of edges. In small bowl, mix granulated sugar and chai spice; sprinkle over butter. Sprinkle with coconut.

3 Unroll remaining can of dough on work surface. Starting at center, press into 12x8-inch rectangle. Place over filling; firmly press edges to seal. Using sharp serrated knife, cut rectangle lengthwise into 8 (12-inch) strips. Twist each strip 7 to 9 times; shape into tight coil. Place 1 coil in each muffin cup. (Muffin cups will be very full.)

4 Bake 20 to 23 minutes or until no longer doughy in center and golden brown. Immediately remove from muffin cups to cooling rack.

5 Meanwhile, in small bowl, stir together powdered sugar and milk until thin enough to drizzle. Drizzle over warm twists. Serve warm.

1 Muffin: Calories 290; Total Fat 11g (Saturated Fat 6g, Trans Fat 0g); Cholesterol 10mg; Sodium 500mg; Total Carbohydrate 45g (Dietary Fiber 0g); Protein 3g **Exchanges:** 1 Starch, 2 Other Carbohydrate, 2 Fat **Carbohydrate Choices:** 3

KITCHEN SECRETS

• Make your own chai spice by combining 1 teaspoon ground cinnamon, 1 teaspoon ground cardamom, ½ teaspoon ground ginger, ¼ teaspoon ground cloves and ¼ teaspoon ground nutmeg.

• For smaller twist muffins, spray 12 regular-size muffin cups. Make dough as directed except cut crosswise into 12 strips. Continue as directed to make 12 muffins.

SWEET BRIE BREAKFAST SANDWICHES

PREP TIME: 30 Minutes | **START TO FINISH:** 50 Minutes | **8 sandwiches**

¼ lb thinly sliced smoked turkey

¼ lb thinly sliced smoked ham

1 can Pillsbury Grands! Flaky Layers Original refrigerated biscuits (8 biscuits)

4 oz Brie cheese, cut into 8 slices (2½x1½x¼-inch thick)

8 thin slices pear (½ medium)

½ cup peach-apricot preserves

1 egg

1 tablespoon water

1 Heat oven to 375°F. Line cookie sheet with cooking parchment paper. Divide turkey and ham into 8 portions. Set aside.

2 Separate dough into 8 biscuits. Using serrated knife, split each biscuit in half horizontally to make 16 biscuits halves. Refrigerate 8 of the biscuit halves.

3 Press remaining biscuit halves into 4-inch rounds. Top each with 1 meat portion, 1 slice cheese, 1 slice pear and 1 tablespoon of the preserves. Remove biscuit halves from refrigerator; press into 4½-inch rounds. Place over filling; press edges to seal. Place 2 inches apart on cookie sheet. Cut 2 small slits in top of each biscuit. Beat egg and water with fork; brush over top of each biscuit.

4 Bake 15 to 20 minutes or until golden brown. Cut sandwiches diagonally in half to serve.

1 Sandwich: Calories 330; Total Fat 12g (Saturated Fat 6g, Trans Fat 0g); Cholesterol 55mg; Sodium 930mg; Total Carbohydrate 42g (Dietary Fiber 1g); Protein 13g **Exchanges:** 1 Starch, 2 Other Carbohydrate, 1 Very Lean Meat, ½Medium-Fat Meat, 1½ Fat **Carbohydrate Choices:** 3

SERVE IT UP

◆ Grab one of these sandwiches and a banana for a quick breakfast on the go.

KITCHEN HACK

FRESHEN UP

Use squeezed lemons to freshen up your garbage disposal. Whirl them for a few seconds and then discard.

BLUEBERRY–CINNAMON ROLL COFFEE CAKE

PREP TIME: 25 Minutes | **START TO FINISH: 1 Hour 15 Minutes** | **8 servings**

1 medium lemon

¼ cup fresh blueberries

¼ cup blueberry preserves

2 teaspoons cold butter, cut into small pieces

2 cans Pillsbury refrigerated cinnamon rolls with cream cheese icing (8 rolls each)

1 egg

¼ cup pecans or cinnamon pecans, coarsely chopped

1. Heat oven to 350°F. Spray nonstick 9-inch tart pan with removable bottom with cooking spray. Line cookie sheet with cooking parchment paper; place tart pan on cookie sheet.

2. In medium bowl, grate 1 teaspoon peel from the lemon. In small bowl, squeeze 1 tablespoon juice from the lemon; set aside.

3. Mix 2 tablespoons of the blueberries with the lemon peel, mashing berries slightly with fork. Stir in preserves, remaining 2 tablespoons blueberries and the butter; set aside.

4. Separate dough into 16 rolls; set aside icing. On parchment paper, press rolls, cinnamon side down, into 3- to 4-inch rounds. Spoon about 1 tablespoon blueberry mixture into center of each round. Fold dough over filling, pressing edges to seal. Place filled rolls in pan seam side up in spoke fashion with 2 in the center.

5. In small bowl, lightly beat egg with whisk; brush over rolls.

6. Bake 22 to 32 minutes or until center is deep golden brown. Cool 5 minutes. Remove side of pan; cool 10 minutes longer. Stir reserved icing into lemon juice. Drizzle evenly over rolls. Sprinkle with pecans. Serve warm or cool.

1 Serving: Calories 370; Total Fat 14g (Saturated Fat 4g, Trans Fat 4g); Cholesterol 25mg; Sodium 700mg; Total Carbohydrate 56g (Dietary Fiber 1g); Protein 5g **Exchanges:** 1½ Starch, 2 Other Carbohydrate, 2½ Fat **Carbohydrate Choices:** 4

KITCHEN HACK

SPEED UP RIPENING

Place underripe avocados, bananas, pears or tomatoes in a small paper bag with an apple or two. The apples emit ethylene gas, which hastens the maturing process of these foods.

LEMON-CREAM CHEESE CRESCENT RING

PREP TIME: 15 Minutes | **START TO FINISH:** 35 Minutes | **6 servings**

CRESCENT RING

- 1 package (8 oz) cream cheese, softened
- ¼ cup granulated sugar
- 2 teaspoons grated lemon peel
- 1 tablespoon fresh lemon juice
- 1 can Pillsbury refrigerated crescent dough sheet

GLAZE

- ½ cup powdered sugar
- 2 to 3 teaspoons milk

1 Heat oven to 350°F. Spray large cookie sheet with cooking spray. In small bowl, mix cream cheese, granulated sugar, lemon peel and lemon juice with electric mixer on medium speed until well blended.

2 Unroll dough on cutting board. Spread cream cheese mixture on rectangle to within ½ inch of edges.

3 Starting with long side of rectangle, roll up; pinch edge to seal. With serrated knife, cut into 12 slices. Arrange slices on cookie sheet in a circle, overlapping slightly.

4 Bake 15 to 20 minutes or until golden brown. In small bowl, mix glaze ingredients until thin enough to drizzle. Drizzle over warm crescent ring.

1 Serving: Calories 250; Total Fat 11g (Saturated Fat 5g, Trans Fat 0g); Cholesterol 15mg; Sodium 350mg; Total Carbohydrate 35g (Dietary Fiber 0g); Protein 3g **Exchanges:** 1 Starch, 1½ Other Carbohydrate, 2 Fat **Carbohydrate Choices:** 2

KITCHEN SECRETS

◆ Sprinkle the crescent ring with powdered sugar in place of the glaze if you like.

◆ You can prepare the crescent ring up to 2 hours ahead through step 3, then cover with plastic wrap and refrigerate. When ready, uncover and bake as directed, adding a few extra minutes to the bake time.

◆ You can use 1 can Pillsbury refrigerated crescent dinner rolls (8 rolls) instead of the dough sheet. Unroll dough and separate into 2 large rectangles. Overlap long sides to form 13 x 7-inch rectangle; firmly press edges and perforations to seal.

CHOCOLATE HAZELNUT CRESCENT RING

PREP TIME: 20 Minutes | **START TO FINISH:** 45 Minutes | 8 servings

1   can Pillsbury refrigerated crescent dough sheet

½   cup hazelnut spread with cocoa (from 13-oz jar)

½   cup finely chopped hazelnuts (filberts), if desired

1   egg, beaten

1   teaspoon coarse sugar or decorator sugar crystals

1. Heat oven to 375°F. Spray large cookie sheet with cooking spray, or line with cooking parchment paper. Unroll dough on work surface. Starting at center, press into 13x8-inch rectangle. Spread hazelnut spread evenly over dough to within ¼ inch of edges. Sprinkle with hazelnuts, reserving 1 tablespoon for topping.

2. Starting with long side, roll up dough; pinch edge to seal. Place seam side down lengthwise in middle of cookie sheet. Using sharp knife, cut dough lengthwise to form 2 halves.

3. Twist halves together with cut sides of dough facing up. Shape into circle; gently pinch ends together. Brush with beaten egg; sprinkle with sugar and reserved hazelnuts.

4. Bake 20 to 22 minutes or until golden brown. Serve warm.

1 Serving: Calories 200; Total Fat 10g (Saturated Fat 2g, Trans Fat 0g); Cholesterol 25mg; Sodium 230mg; Total Carbohydrate 25g (Dietary Fiber 1g); Protein 4g **Exchanges:** 1½ Other Carbohydrate, ½ Medium-Fat Meat, 1½ Fat **Carbohydrate Choices:** 1½

KITCHEN SECRETS

◆ You can use almonds in place of the hazelnuts if you like.

◆ Keep the dough well chilled for this recipe. If dough becomes warm, place in refrigerator for easier handling.

CINNAMON FRENCH TOAST BAKE

PREP TIME: 15 Minutes | **START TO FINISH:** 1 Hour | **12 servings**

¼ cup butter, melted

2 cans Pillsbury refrigerated cinnamon rolls with icing (8 rolls each)

6 eggs

½ cup whipping cream

2 teaspoons ground cinnamon

2 teaspoons vanilla

1 cup chopped pecans

1 cup real maple syrup

1 Heat oven to 375°F. Into ungreased 13x9-inch (3-quart) glass baking dish, pour butter. Separate dough into 16 rolls; set aside icing. Cut each roll into 8 pieces; place pieces in baking dish.

2 In medium bowl, beat eggs. Beat in cream, cinnamon and vanilla until well blended; gently pour over roll pieces. Sprinkle with pecans; drizzle with syrup.

3 Bake 20 to 28 minutes or until golden brown. Cool 15 minutes.

4 Meanwhile, remove covers from icing; microwave on Medium (50%) 10 to 15 seconds or until thin enough to drizzle.

5 Drizzle icing over top. If desired, spoon syrup from dish over individual servings.

1 Serving: Calories 440; Total Fat 23g (Saturated Fat 10g, Trans Fat 0g); Cholesterol 115mg; Sodium 530mg; Total Carbohydrate 53g (Dietary Fiber 2g); Protein 7g **Exchanges:** 1 Starch, 2½ Other Carbohydrate, ½ High-Fat Meat, 3½ Fat **Carbohydrate Choices:** 3½

SERVE IT UP

◆ Make this decadent morning casserole a meal by serving it with breakfast sausage, orange juice and fresh berries.

◆ Serve with additional maple syrup.

ADD A GARNISH

◆ After drizzling with icing, sprinkle with powdered sugar if you like. To control the sprinkle, place a teaspoon or two of powdered sugar in a small fine-mesh strainer. Tap the edge of the strainer with a spoon over the casserole.

CINNAMON PULL-APART

PREP TIME: 25 Minutes | **START TO FINISH:** 1 Hour 5 Minutes | **12 servings**

½ cup granulated sugar

1 teaspoon ground cinnamon

2 cans Pillsbury Grands!™ Homestyle refrigerated buttermilk biscuits (8 biscuits each)

¾ cup packed brown sugar

½ cup butter, melted

1. Heat oven to 350°F. Spray 12-cup fluted tube cake pan with cooking spray.

2. In large resealable food-storage plastic bag, mix granulated sugar and cinnamon. Separate dough into 16 biscuits; cut each into 4 pieces. Place pieces in bag and shake to coat. Arrange pieces in pan. In small bowl, mix brown sugar and butter until well blended; pour over biscuit pieces.

3. Bake 30 to 35 minutes or until golden brown and no longer doughy in center. Cool 5 minutes. Carefully run knife or spatula around pan to loosen. Turn upside down onto serving plate; pull apart to serve. Serve warm.

1 Serving: Calories 390; Total Fat 16g (Saturated Fat 8g, Trans Fat 0g); Cholesterol 20mg; Sodium 660mg; Total Carbohydrate 57g (Dietary Fiber 0g); Protein 5g **Exchanges:** 1½ Starch, 2½ Other Carbohydrate, 3 Fat **Carbohydrate Choices:** 4

KITCHEN SECRET

◆ For the best results, keep the biscuit dough in the refrigerator until just before you use it. Warm dough might get sticky and be hard to handle.

PUMPKIN SPICE PULL-APART

PREP TIME: 15 Minutes | **START TO FINISH: 1 Hour 5 Minutes** | **8 servings**

¼ cup granulated sugar

1¼ teaspoons pumpkin pie spice

1 can Pillsbury Grands! Flaky Layers refrigerated honey butter biscuits (8 biscuits)

2 tablespoons butter, melted

¾ cup canned pumpkin pie mix (not plain pumpkin)

½ cup powdered sugar

2 to 3 teaspoons milk

1 teaspoon vanilla

1 Heat oven to 350°F. Spray 9x5-inch loaf pan with cooking spray. In small bowl, mix granulated sugar and 1 teaspoon of the pumpkin pie spice.

2 Separate dough into 8 biscuits. Separate each biscuit into 2 layers, making total of 16 biscuit rounds. Brush cut side of each biscuit round with melted butter. Spread slightly less than 1 tablespoon pumpkin pie mix on top of each. Sprinkle rounds with spice-sugar mixture.

3 Stack biscuits in 4 piles of 4 biscuit rounds each. Place stacks on their sides in single row in loaf pan, making sure sides without filling are on both ends touching pan.

4 Bake 40 to 45 minutes or until deep golden brown and center is baked through.

5 Cool 10 minutes. Turn pan upside down on serving platter. In small bowl, mix powdered sugar, milk, vanilla and remaining ¼ teaspoon pumpkin pie spice until thin enough to drizzle. Drizzle over warm loaf. Serve warm.

1 Serving: Calories 260; Total Fat 9g (Saturated Fat 4.5g, Trans Fat 0g); Cholesterol 10mg; Sodium 460mg; Total Carbohydrate 42g (Dietary Fiber 1g); Protein 3g **Exchanges:** 1 Starch, 2 Other Carbohydrate, 1½ Fat **Carbohydrate Choices:** 3

KITCHEN SECRETS

◆ The pumpkin pie mix used in this recipe is not the same as canned pumpkin. Pumpkin pie mix contains a blend of traditional spices as well as sugar. Regular canned pumpkin does not contain salt, sugar or spices.

◆ You can assemble the loaf as directed up to a day in advance. Cover with plastic wrap and refrigerate until ready to bake. Bake as directed in recipe.

ADD A GARNISH

◆ For more of a fall flavor, serve this loaf with a side of pumpkin butter.

TOASTER STRUDEL HACKS

Try one of these fun takes on Pillsbury Toaster Strudel™.

MAKE A FACE

Using the glaze for glue, attach pieces of fruit and nuts to the strudel to make a face.

NUTS FOR CHOCOLATE

Spread the glaze on the strudel and let it dry. Spread a thin layer of hazelnut spread over the glaze. Use a toothpick to draw decorations through the toppings.

PARTY UP

After decorating with glaze, add your favorite sprinkles to get your par-day started!

PLAY A GAME

Cut strudels crosswise into thirds. Use the glaze to add dots to the pieces like dominoes. Have fun matching up the dots.

TIC-TAC-TOE

Breakfast will be fun when you use the glaze to play tic-tac-toe.

SAVORY BREADS

EASY ASIAGO OLIVE ROLLS

PREP TIME: 10 Minutes | **START TO FINISH:** 30 Minutes | **10 rolls**

1 can Pillsbury refrigerated classic pizza crust

¼ cup refrigerated olive tapenade

½ cup grated Asiago cheese

1 teaspoon chopped fresh rosemary leaves

1 tablespoon butter, melted

1 Heat oven to 450°F. Spray 9-inch round cake pan with cooking spray.

2 On lightly floured cutting board, unroll dough. Spread olive tapenade over dough to within ¼ inch of edge. Sprinkle with cheese and rosemary. Starting at long side, gently roll up dough. Using a serrated knife, cut into 10 (¼-inch-thick) slices. Place slices in cake pan. Brush tops with melted butter.

3 Bake 15 to 20 minutes or until golden. Serve warm.

1 Roll: Calories 130; Total Fat 4.5g (Saturated Fat 2g, Trans Fat 0g); Cholesterol 0mg; Sodium 440mg; Total Carbohydrate 19g (Dietary Fiber 0g); Protein 4g **Exchanges:** 1 Starch, 1 Fat **Carbohydrate Choices:** 1

SERVE IT UP

◆ Pair these flavorful rolls with spaghetti or rigatoni for a fun change-up from the typical garlic bread.

KITCHEN HACK

WARM BISCUITS OR ROLLS

Place on a microwavable plate or in a napkin-lined nonmetal basket.
For 1 biscuit or roll, microwave 5 to 10 seconds; for 4 biscuits or rolls, microwave 20 to 30 seconds.

PARMESAN DILL CRESCENTS

PREP TIME: 10 Minutes | **START TO FINISH:** 25 Minutes | 8 rolls

1   can Pillsbury refrigerated
     crescent dinner rolls (8 rolls)

1   tablespoon plus 1 teaspoon
     grated Parmesan cheese

1   tablespoon finely chopped
     red bell pepper, if desired

1¼   teaspoons dried dill weed

1   Heat oven to 375°F. Unroll dough; separate into 8 triangles.

2   In small bowl, mix 1 tablespoon of the Parmesan cheese, bell pepper and
     1 teaspoon of the dill weed. Sprinkle evenly over each triangle. Roll loosely
     from shortest side of triangle to opposite point. Place rolls, point side down,
     on ungreased cookie sheet; curve into crescent shape. In small bowl, mix
     remaining 1 teaspoon Parmesan cheese and ¼ teaspoon dill weed; sprinkle
     evenly over crescents.

3   Bake at 375°F. for 11 to 13 minutes or until golden brown.

1 roll: Calories 110; Total Fat 5g (Saturated Fat 2g, Trans Fat 0g); Cholesterol 0mg; Sodium 230mg; Total
Carbohydrate 12g (Dietary Fiber 0g); Protein 2g **Exchanges:** ½ Starch, ½ Other Carbohydrate, 1 Fat
Carbohydrate Choices: 1

CRESCENT ROLLS WITH FRESH HERBS

PREP TIME: 25 Minutes | **START TO FINISH:** 40 Minutes | **16 rolls**

4 teaspoons finely chopped fresh parsley

4 teaspoons finely chopped fresh thyme leaves

4 teaspoons finely chopped fresh basil leaves

4 teaspoons finely chopped fresh oregano leaves

2 cans Pillsbury refrigerated crescent dinner rolls (8 rolls each)

1 egg

1 teaspoon water

1 Heat oven to 375°F. In small bowl, mix all chopped herbs.

2 Separate dough into 16 triangles. Sprinkle each triangle with 1 teaspoon herb mixture; press lightly into dough. Starting at shortest side, roll up to opposite point. On ungreased cookie sheets, place rolls point side down; curve each into crescent shape.

3 In small bowl, beat egg and water until blended. Brush egg mixture over tops of rolls.

4 Bake 10 to 12 minutes or until golden brown. Serve warm.

1 Roll: Calories 110; Total Fat 6g (Saturated Fat 2g, Trans Fat 1.5g); Cholesterol 15mg; Sodium 220mg; Total Carbohydrate 11g (Dietary Fiber 0g); Protein 2g **Exchanges:** 1 Starch, 1 Fat **Carbohydrate Choices:** 1

KITCHEN SECRETS

◆ About ⅓ cup of any one herb or a combination of herbs can be substituted for the four herbs in this recipe.

◆ Use a kitchen scissors to quickly chop the fresh herbs.

ADD A GARNISH

◆ Dress up these rolls with a small fresh herb leaf on each one. After brushing rolls with egg mixture, place 1 herb leaf on top of each roll; brush egg mixture over top of leaf. Bake as directed.

BACON BREADSTICK FOCACCIA

PREP TIME: 15 Minutes | **START TO FINISH:** 40 Minutes | 6 servings

1   can Pillsbury refrigerated original breadsticks (12 breadsticks)

11 slices packaged precooked bacon (from 2.1-oz package)

1   egg, beaten

1   Heat oven to 375°F. Unroll dough; separate into 12 strips.

2   Chop 1 slice of the bacon; set aside. Starting at center of ungreased cookie sheet, coil remaining 10 bacon slices with the dough strips into a loose spiral, pinching ends together securely as strips are added.

3   Drizzle or brush egg over dough, using all of egg to fill crevices. Sprinkle with chopped bacon.

4   Bake 20 to 25 minutes or until edges are deep golden brown. Cut into wedges; serve warm.

1 Serving: Calories 220; Total Fat 8g (Saturated Fat 2g, Trans Fat 0g); Cholesterol 45mg; Sodium 540mg; Total Carbohydrate 26g (Dietary Fiber 0g); Protein 10g **Exchanges:** 2 Starch, ½ High-Fat Meat, ½ Fat **Carbohydrate Choices:** 2

KITCHEN SECRET

◆ Precooked bacon is needed for this recipe so it will be fully cooked by the time the bread bakes. It also has less fat than regular bacon, so the bread won't be greasy. Look for boxes of precooked bacon near the regular bacon and packaged lunch meat at the supermarket.

ADD A GARNISH

◆ Sprinkle ½ teaspoon chopped parsley over the bread before baking for splash of color.

KITCHEN HACK

CREATIVE USES

Leftover biscuits or rolls can be crumbled or broken up to be used to top soup or chili or coarsely chopped to add to salads.

CHEESY SURPRISE CORNBREAD BISCUITS

PREP TIME: 25 Minutes | **START TO FINISH:** 40 Minutes | **10 biscuits**

2 cans Pillsbury Grands! Juniors Flaky Layers™ refrigerated buttermilk biscuits (5 biscuits each)

2 sticks (1 oz each) mozzarella string cheese, each cut crosswise into 5 pieces

3 tablespoons butter, melted

¼ cup cornmeal

2 teaspoons sugar

½ teaspoon red pepper flakes

1 Heat oven to 375°F. Spray 10 regular-size muffin cups with cooking spray. Separate dough into 10 biscuits; separate each biscuit into 2 layers. On bottom layer of each biscuit, place 1 piece of cheese; place top layer over cheese and press edges together to seal.

2 Place melted butter in shallow bowl. In another shallow bowl, mix cornmeal, sugar and pepper flakes. Dip each filled biscuit into butter; coat lightly with cornmeal mixture. Place in muffin cup.

3 Bake 10 to 14 minutes or until light golden brown. If necessary, run knife around edge of each muffin cup; remove biscuits from cups. Serve warm.

1 Biscuit: Calories 170; Total Fat 8g (Saturated Fat 4.5g, Trans Fat 0g); Cholesterol 15mg; Sodium 370mg; Total Carbohydrate 19g (Dietary Fiber 0g); Protein 3g **Exchanges:** 1 Starch, ½ Other Carbohydrate, 1½ Fat **Carbohydrate Choices:** 1

KITCHEN SECRET

◆ Like your cornbread biscuits nice and sweet? Increase the sugar to 1 tablespoon.

KITCHEN HACK

CUTTING BISCUITS

Use a sharp knife, kitchen shears or pizza cutter to quickly cut biscuits into pieces for recipes that use dough pieces.

MUSTARD PRETZEL BREADSTICKS

PREP TIME: 15 Minutes | **START TO FINISH:** 30 Minutes | 12 breadsticks

3 cups water

2 tablespoons baking soda

1 can Pillsbury refrigerated breadsticks (12 breadsticks)

1 tablespoon spicy brown mustard

1 teaspoon mustard seed

¾ teaspoon dried oregano leaves

1 Heat oven to 375°F. Line large cookie sheet with cooking parchment paper.

2 In 10-inch skillet, heat water and baking soda to boiling over high heat. Reduce heat to simmer. Meanwhile, unroll dough; separate at perforations into 12 breadsticks. Roll each breadstick into a rope 8 inches long.

3 Carefully place 2 breadsticks into water mixture; cook 15 seconds. Using slotted spoon, remove breadsticks and arrange on cookie sheet about 1 inch apart. Repeat with remaining breadsticks.

4 Brush breadsticks with mustard. Sprinkle with mustard seed and oregano.

5 Bake 14 to 16 minutes or until golden brown. Carefully peel breadsticks from parchment paper. Serve warm.

1 Breadstick: Calories 70; Total Fat 1g (Saturated Fat 0g, Trans Fat 0g); Cholesterol 0mg; Sodium 260mg; Total Carbohydrate 13g (Dietary Fiber 0g); Protein 2g **Exchanges:** 1 Starch **Carbohydrate Choices:** 1

KITCHEN SECRETS

◆ If you like, skip the shaping and just use the breadsticks as they are. Or, for a fancy take on these, roll each breadstick to 10 inches and tie it into a knot before boiling.

◆ What kind of mustard do you have on hand? You can also use Dijon or honey mustard if you prefer. Serve up some extra mustard on the side for dipping.

STUFFED CRESCENT ROLL CARROTS

PREP TIME: 35 Minutes | **START TO FINISH:** 45 Minutes | **8 servings**

8 (12x4-inch) sheets of foil

1 can Pillsbury refrigerated crescent dinner rolls (8 rolls)

1 package (8 oz) cream cheese, softened

¼ cup chopped fresh parsley

¼ cup chopped fresh chives

1 teaspoon grated lemon peel

¼ teaspoon salt

16 small sprigs fresh parsley

1. Heat oven to 400°F. Roll sheets of foil from shorter ends into cone-shaped molds. Unroll dough on cutting board; press perforations to seal. Use pizza cutter or knife to cut dough lengthwise into 8 (1-inch) strips.

2. Wrap 1 strip around each foil mold to create carrot shape. Place 1 inch apart on ungreased cookie sheet.

3. Bake 7 to 9 minutes or until golden brown. Remove to cooling rack; cool completely. Remove foil molds.

4. In medium bowl, beat cream cheese, parsley, chives, lemon peel and salt with electric mixer on medium speed until smooth and combined. Pipe or spoon cream cheese mixture into cavity of each crescent. Top with 2 sprigs parsley for carrot top.

1 Serving: Calories 200; Total Fat 15g (Saturated Fat 7g, Trans Fat 0g); Cholesterol 30mg; Sodium 390mg; Total Carbohydrate 14g (Dietary Fiber 0g); Protein 4g **Exchanges:** 1 Starch, 3 Fat **Carbohydrate Choices:** 1

KITCHEN SECRETS

◆ Gently twist foil molds for easier removal from crescents.

◆ Swap the cream cheese mixture with your own favorite filling, such as egg salad or chicken salad.

◆ You can substitute 1 can Pillsbury refrigerated crescent dough sheet for the crescent rolls. Just unroll dough and prepare as directed.

CHEESY ROSEMARY MONKEY BREAD ROLLS

PREP TIME: 15 Minutes | **START TO FINISH:** 40 Minutes | 12 rolls

2 cans Pillsbury refrigerated crescent dinner rolls (8 rolls each)

3 tablespoons butter, melted

1 teaspoon chopped fresh rosemary leaves

¾ teaspoon garlic powder

1 cup shredded Colby–Monterey Jack cheese blend (4 oz)

1 Heat oven to 350°F. Spray 12 regular-size muffin cups with cooking spray.

2 Unroll each can of dough into 1 large rectangle on cutting board; press perforations to seal. Cut each rectangle into 8 rows by 3 rows to make 24 pieces each, 48 pieces total. Roll each piece into a ball.

3 In small bowl, mix melted butter, rosemary and garlic powder. Roll each ball in butter mixture. Place 4 balls in each muffin cup.

4 Bake 17 to 19 minutes or until golden brown and no longer doughy in center. Sprinkle cheese evenly in each cup. Bake 3 to 5 minutes longer or until cheese is melted. Let stand 1 minute. Remove from pan. Serve warm.

1 Roll: Calories 200; Total Fat 14g (Saturated Fat 7g, Trans Fat 0g); Cholesterol 15mg; Sodium 370mg; Total Carbohydrate 15g (Dietary Fiber 0g); Protein 3g **Exchanges:** 1 Starch, 2½ Fat **Carbohydrate Choices:** 1

KITCHEN SECRETS

◆ Be sure to chop the rosemary leaves instead of leaving them whole. They can become dry quickly during baking.

◆ You can substitute 2 cans Pillsbury refrigerated crescent dough sheet (1 sheet each) for the crescent rolls. Just unroll dough and cut as directed.

KITCHEN HACK

SPIN DRY

Quickly dry sprigs of fresh herbs using your salad spinner.

Clockwise from top:
Greek Monkey Bread (page 123)
Gruyère Monkey Bread
Rolls (page 122)
Cheesy Rosemary Monkey Bread
Rolls (left)

GRUYÈRE MONKEY BREAD ROLLS

PREP TIME: 15 Minutes | **START TO FINISH:** 40 Minutes | 8 rolls

3   tablespoons butter, melted

2   teaspoons chopped fresh thyme leaves

1   can Pillsbury Grands! Flaky Layers refrigerated buttermilk biscuits (8 biscuits)

4   oz Gruyère cheese, shredded (1 cup)

1. Heat oven to 375°F. Spray 8 regular-size muffin cups with cooking spray.

2. In medium bowl, mix butter and thyme until blended.

3. Separate dough into 8 biscuits; cut each into 8 pieces. Add pieces to butter mixture; toss to coat. In each muffin cup, place 4 biscuit pieces and sprinkle with 1 tablespoon cheese. Top with 4 more biscuit pieces.

4. Bake 14 to 18 minutes or until golden brown and no longer doughy in center. Sprinkle remaining cheese over rolls. Bake 3 to 4 minutes longer or until cheese is melted. Cool 1 minute. Remove from muffin cups. Serve warm.

1 Roll: Calories 270; Total Fat 15g (Saturated Fat 8g, Trans Fat 0g); Cholesterol 25mg; Sodium 590mg; Total Carbohydrate 26g (Dietary Fiber 0g); Protein 8g **Exchanges:** 1½ Starch, ½ High-Fat Meat, 2 Fat **Carbohydrate Choices:** 2

KITCHEN SECRET

◆ Any of your favorite fresh herbs or a blend of fresh herbs can be substituted for the thyme in this recipe. Try basil or rosemary.

SERVE IT UP

◆ Serve these rolls for any special occasion or holiday meal.

KITCHEN HACK

MEASURE FIRST

If there's a lot happening while you are baking that makes you easily distracted, measure all your ingredients first before mixing to be sure you don't forget any.

GREEK MONKEY BREAD

PREP TIME: 25 Minutes | **START TO FINISH:** 1 Hour 15 Minutes | 8 servings

- 2 tablespoons olive oil
- 2 tablespoons chopped fresh Italian parsley
- 1 teaspoon dried oregano leaves
- 2 cloves garlic, finely chopped
- 1 can Pillsbury refrigerated classic pizza crust
- 1 cup shredded Italian cheese blend or mozzarella cheese (4 oz)
- 2 tablespoons drained chopped sun-dried tomatoes in olive oil, patted dry
- 2 tablespoons chopped pitted kalamata olives
- 2 tablespoons crumbled feta cheese

1 Heat oven to 375°F. Spray 8x4-inch loaf pan with cooking spray. Line pan with cooking parchment paper, allowing paper to hang 2 inches over long sides of pan. In 1-gallon resealable food-storage plastic bag, combine oil, parsley, oregano and garlic; mix well.

2 Using pizza cutter, cut dough into 1-inch pieces; shape each into a ball. Place balls in bag; seal bag and shake to coat evenly. Arrange half of the balls in bottom of loaf pan. Sprinkle with one-half each of the Italian cheese blend, tomatoes, olives and feta cheese. Arrange remaining balls on top, and sprinkle with remaining Italian cheese blend, tomatoes, olives and feta cheese.

3 Bake 30 to 35 minutes or until deep golden brown and no longer doughy in center. Cool 10 minutes. Remove from pan. Serve warm.

1 Serving: Calories 210; Total Fat 9g (Saturated Fat 3.5g, Trans Fat 0g); Cholesterol 15mg; Sodium 430mg; Total Carbohydrate 25g (Dietary Fiber 0g); Protein 7g **Exchanges:** 1 Starch, ½ Other Carbohydrate, ½ High-Fat Meat, 1 Fat **Carbohydrate Choices:** 1½

KITCHEN SECRET

◆ Lining the pan with parchment paper may seem like an unnecessary step, but the paper makes this cheesy bread come out of the pan easily and makes cleanup a snap.

SERVE IT UP

◆ This bread makes a delicious accompaniment to minestrone, cream of broccoli or any other vegetable-packed soup.

KITCHEN HACK

QUICK CHOP

To chop fresh basil leaves quickly, lay several leaves on top of one another and then roll lengthwise before slicing them crosswise.

JALAPEÑO AND CHEESE-FILLED PRETZELS

PREP TIME: 30 Minutes | **START TO FINISH:** 50 Minutes | **4 pretzels**

FILLING

- 3 oz cream cheese, softened (from 8-oz package)
- ½ cup finely shredded Cheddar cheese (2 oz)
- 1 tablespoon finely chopped pickled jalapeño chile slices (from 12-oz jar)

PRETZELS

- 1 can Pillsbury refrigerated classic pizza crust
- 2 cups water
- ¼ cup baking soda
- 1 egg
- 1 tablespoon water
  Coarse (kosher or sea) salt

1. Heat oven to 400°F. In small bowl, mix filling ingredients; set aside. Line large cookie sheet with cooking parchment paper. On lightly floured cutting board, unroll dough. Starting at center, press dough into 14x12-inch rectangle. Cut lengthwise into 4 strips.

2. Spoon about ¼ cup of the filling onto long edge of each dough strip. Stretch dough over filling; brush edges with water and pinch to seal. Pick up ends of filled dough, and stretch to make 24-inch rope.

3. To make pretzel shape, form each rope into U shape. Twist ends twice. Press down where dough overlaps in an X to hold shape. Pick up ends and fold over so they rest over bottom of U shape.

4. In medium microwavable bowl, microwave 2 cups water uncovered on High about 2 minutes or until hot. Add baking soda; stir until dissolved. Dip each pretzel, 1 at a time, into water mixture. Immediately remove from water with large pancake turner; let stand about 5 minutes. In small bowl, beat egg and 1 tablespoon water with whisk; brush pretzels with egg mixture. Place pretzels on cookie sheet; sprinkle with salt.

5. Bake 11 to 15 minutes or until tops of pretzels are dark golden brown.

1 Pretzel: Calories 400; Total Fat 16g (Saturated Fat 8g, Trans Fat 0g); Cholesterol 85mg; Sodium 3400mg; Total Carbohydrate 49g (Dietary Fiber 2g); Protein 14g **Exchanges:** 1 Starch, 2½ Other Carbohydrate, 1½ High-Fat Meat, ½ Fat **Carbohydrate Choices:** 3

SERVE IT UP

◆ Serve these filled pretzels with your favorite salsa or queso dip.

KITCHEN HACK

FRESH OUT

If you don't have any fresh herbs available, substitute dried herbs using one-third of the amount of fresh: 1 tablespoon fresh herbs = 1 teaspoon dried herbs.

Clockwise from top:
Dill Pickle Pull-Apart (right)
Cheese-Stuffed Pull-Apart (page 128)
Reuben Pull-Apart (page 129)

DILL PICKLE PULL-APART

PREP TIME: 20 Minutes | **START TO FINISH:** 1 Hour 20 Minutes | 8 servings

3   tablespoons butter, melted

1   teaspoon dill pickle juice

¼   teaspoon crushed red pepper flakes

¼   teaspoon garlic powder

1   can Pillsbury Grands! Flaky Layers refrigerated buttermilk biscuits

1   cup shredded sharp Cheddar cheese (4 oz)

24 dill pickle slices (about ½ cup), drained

1   Heat oven to 350°F. Spray 9x5-inch loaf pan with cooking spray. Line pan with cooking parchment paper, allowing paper to hang 2 inches over long sides of pan.

2   In small bowl, combine butter, dill pickle juice, pepper flakes and garlic powder.

3   Separate dough into 8 biscuits; separate each biscuit into 2 layers. Brush both sides of each biscuit with melted butter mixture. Top half of the biscuits with 1 tablespoon Cheddar cheese and 3 pickle slices. Place remaining biscuit halves on top of pickles; press edges to seal. Starting at one short end of pan, place biscuit layers on their edges, just touching each other, until pan is loosely filled. Brush with remaining melted butter mixture.

4   Bake 35 to 40 minutes or until cheese is melted and biscuits are golden brown. Sprinkle with remaining ½ cup cheese. Bake 3 to 4 minutes longer or until cheese is melted. Cool 10 minutes; remove from pan to cooling rack, using parchment paper as handles. Cool 10 minutes.

1 Serving: Calories 270; Total Fat 15g (Saturated Fat 8g, Trans Fat 0g); Cholesterol 25mg; Sodium 750mg; Total Carbohydrate 27g (Dietary Fiber 0g); Protein 7g **Exchanges:** 1 Starch, 1 Other Carbohydrate, ½ High-Fat Meat, 2 Fat **Carbohydrate Choices:** 2

KITCHEN SECRET

◆ For more pickle flavor, sprinkle chopped dill pickles on top of the cheese before returning to oven to melt the cheese.

SERVE IT UP

◆ Serve this delicious pickle bread with your favorite chili or soup or as an appetizer for game day.

CHEESE-STUFFED PULL-APART

PREP TIME: 10 Minutes | **START TO FINISH:** 30 Minutes | 10 servings

½ cup grated Parmesan cheese

½ teaspoon Italian seasoning

2 cans Pillsbury Grands! Flaky Layers refrigerated buttermilk biscuits (5 biscuits each)

10 cubes (¾ inch) Cheddar, Monterey Jack or mozzarella cheese

3 tablespoons butter, melted

1 Heat oven to 375°F. Spray 8-inch round pan with cooking spray. In small bowl, stir together Parmesan cheese and Italian seasoning.

2 Separate dough into 10 biscuits; press each into 2-inch round. Place 1 cheese cube in center of each biscuit round. Bring dough up around cheese cube; press edges to seal and shape into a ball. Roll in butter, then in Parmesan cheese mixture. Place balls ¼ inch apart in pan.

3 Bake 15 to 20 minutes or until golden brown. Cool slightly before serving.

1 Serving: Calories 260; Total Fat 13g (Saturated Fat 7g, Trans Fat 0g); Cholesterol 20mg; Sodium 600mg; Total Carbohydrate 26g (Dietary Fiber 0g); Protein 7g **Exchanges:** 1½ Starch, ½ Medium-Fat Meat, 2 Fat **Carbohydrate Choices:** 2

SERVE IT UP

◆ Dunk pieces of this savory bread into heated pizza or marinara sauce for a delicious variation.

KITCHEN HACK

NO SHELLS

Crack your eggs one at a time on the edge of the counter using one good tap to create one crack in the center. Open the egg into a small dish before adding it to other ingredients so you can scoop out any shell pieces that fell into the egg.

REUBEN PULL-APART

PREP TIME: 15 Minutes | **START TO FINISH:** 1 Hour 25 Minutes | **16 servings**

½ cup shredded Swiss cheese (2 oz)

½ cup finely chopped corned beef (about 2½ oz)

½ cup sauerkraut (from 8-oz can), drained, squeezed

1 can Pillsbury Grands! Flaky Layers refrigerated buttermilk biscuits (8 biscuits)

2 tablespoons butter, melted

¼ cup sliced green onions with tops

½ cup Thousand Island dressing

1 Heat oven to 350°F. Spray 9x5-inch loaf pan with cooking spray. Line pan with cooking parchment paper, allowing paper to hang 2 inches over long sides of pan.

2 In medium bowl, combine cheese, corned beef and sauerkraut; set aside. Separate dough into 8 biscuits; separate each biscuit in half. Spoon about 1 tablespoon cheese mixture onto each of 8 biscuit halves, Top with second biscuit half and 1 tablespoon cheese mixture, pressing cheese mixture lightly into biscuit. Starting at one short end of pan, place biscuit layers on their edges, just touching each other, until pan is loosely filled. Sprinkle any remaining cheese mixture between biscuits. Brush with butter; sprinkle with onions.

3 Bake 45 to 50 minutes or until golden brown and no longer doughy in center. Cover loosely with foil during last 10 minutes of bake time to prevent overbrowning if necessary.

4 Cool 10 minutes. Remove from pan to cooling rack, using parchment paper as handles. Cool 10 minutes longer. Serve with dressing.

1 Serving: Calories 150; Total Fat 8g (Saturated Fat 3.5g, Trans Fat 0g); Cholesterol 10mg; Sodium 460mg; Total Carbohydrate 14g (Dietary Fiber 0g); Protein 4g **Exchanges:** 1 Starch, 1½ Fat **Carbohydrate Choices:** 1

KITCHEN SECRET

◆ Sprinkle the dough with ¼ teaspoon caraway seed for a more intense Reuben flavor.

SERVE IT UP

◆ Try serving this savory bread alongside a Cobb salad or creamy potato chowder.

GARLIC, PARMESAN AND RED PEPPER LOAF

PREP TIME: 5 Minutes | **START TO FINISH:** 40 Minutes | **6 slices**

1 can Pillsbury refrigerated crusty French loaf

1 tablespoon butter, melted

¼ teaspoon crushed red pepper flakes

¼ teaspoon garlic salt

2 tablespoons shredded Parmesan cheese

1 Heat oven to 350°F. Spray cookie sheet with cooking spray. Place dough seam side down on cookie sheet.

2 Cut slit or slashes in dough as directed on can. In small bowl, mix melted butter, pepper flakes and garlic salt. Brush on top of dough.

3 Bake 25 to 30 minutes or until deep golden brown, topping with cheese during last 5 minutes of baking. Cool 5 minutes before slicing.

1 Slice: Calories 150; Total Fat 4g (Saturated Fat 2g, Trans Fat 0g); Cholesterol 5mg; Sodium 400mg; Total Carbohydrate 24g (Dietary Fiber 0g); Protein 5g **Exchanges:** 1½ Starch, ½ Fat **Carbohydrate Choices:** 1½

SERVE IT UP

◆ Serve slices of this bread with olive oil for dipping. It pairs perfectly with roasted chicken and squash for an autumn meal.

KITCHEN HACK

TONGUE TANTALIZING

To keep rolls, breadsticks and crescents having the best texture, remove them immediately from the cookie sheet to a cooling rack, and serve warm unless otherwise noted in the recipe.

SEA SALT AND CRACKED BLACK PEPPER ITALIAN LOAF

PREP TIME: 5 Minutes | **START TO FINISH:** 40 Minutes | **6 slices**

1 can Pillsbury refrigerated crusty French loaf

1 tablespoon butter, melted

½ to 1 teaspoon coarse sea salt

¼ teaspoon cracked black pepper

1 Heat oven to 350°F. Spray a cookie sheet with cooking spray. Place dough seam side down on cookie sheet.

2 Cut slit or slashes in dough as directed on can. Brush with melted butter. Sprinkle with salt and pepper.

3 Bake 25 to 30 minutes or until deep golden brown. Cool 5 minutes before slicing.

1 Slice: Calories 140; Total Fat 3g (Saturated Fat 1g, Trans Fat 0g); Cholesterol 5mg; Sodium 440mg; Total Carbohydrate 24g (Dietary Fiber 0g); Protein 4g **Exchanges:** 1½ Starch, ½ Fat **Carbohydrate Choices:** 1½

ADD A GARNISH

◆ For added flavor, try topping with chopped fresh or dried herbs.

STUFFED MOZZARELLA GARLIC BREAD

PREP TIME: 5 Minutes | **START TO FINISH:** 40 Minutes | **6 slices**

1   can Pillsbury refrigerated crusty French loaf

1   tablespoon butter, melted

¼   teaspoon garlic salt

⅓   cup shredded mozzarella cheese

1   Heat oven to 350°F. Line cookie sheet with foil. Place dough seam side down on cookie sheet.

2   Using sharp knife, cut half-inch-deep slashes 1 inch apart in top of dough. In small bowl, mix melted butter and garlic salt. Brush on top of dough. Insert cheese into each slash.

3   Bake 25 to 27 minutes or until deep golden brown and cheese is bubbly. Cool 5 minutes before slicing.

1 Slice: Calories 160; Total Fat 4.5g (Saturated Fat 2.5g, Trans Fat 0g); Cholesterol 10mg; Sodium 400mg; Total Carbohydrate 24g (Dietary Fiber 0g); Protein 5g **Exchanges:** 1 Starch, ½ Other Carbohydrate, 1 Fat **Carbohydrate Choices:** 1½

KITCHEN HACK

CHILLED IS BEST

Always take your Pillsbury dough out of the refrigerator just when you are ready to use it. It is easiest to work with and performs the best when it's cold.

EVERYTHING BAGEL FRENCH BREAD

PREP TIME: 5 Minutes | **START TO FINISH:** 40 Minutes | **6 slices**

1   can Pillsbury refrigerated crusty French loaf

1   tablespoon butter, melted

1   teaspoon dried chopped onion

1   teaspoon dried minced garlic

1   teaspoon poppy seed

1   teaspoon sesame seed

¼   teaspoon salt

1   Heat oven to 350°F. Spray cookie sheet with cooking spray. Place dough seam side down on cookie sheet.

2   Cut slit or slashes in dough as directed on can. Brush with melted butter. In small bowl, mix onion, garlic, poppy seed and sesame seed. Sprinkle on top of dough; sprinkle with salt.

3   Bake 25 to 30 minutes or until deep golden brown. Cool 5 minutes before slicing.

1 Slice: Calories 150; Total Fat 4g (Saturated Fat 2g, Trans Fat 0g); Cholesterol 5mg; Sodium 420mg; Total Carbohydrate 25g (Dietary Fiber 0g); Protein 4g **Exchanges:** 1½ Starch, ½ Fat **Carbohydrate Choices:** 1½

KITCHEN SECRET

◆ Store leftovers tightly covered, and eat within 3 days.

ASIAGO CHEESE AND ONION BRAID

PREP TIME: 25 Minutes | **START TO FINISH:** 45 Minutes | **12 slices**

2 tablespoons butter

1 large sweet onion, cut in half, thinly sliced (about 2 cups)

1 tablespoon packed brown sugar

1 teaspoon dried thyme leaves

1 can Pillsbury refrigerated classic pizza crust

1 cup shredded Asiago cheese (4 oz)

1 egg white, beaten

½ teaspoon poppy seed

KITCHEN SECRET

◆ Mozzarella or fontina cheese can be used in place of the Asiago.

SERVE IT UP

◆ Serve this braid as an appetizer or alongside a soup or salad.

1 Heat oven to 425°F. Spray large cookie sheet with cooking spray.

2 In 10-inch skillet, melt butter over medium heat. Add onion; cook about 15 minutes, stirring occasionally, until onion is golden brown. Stir in brown sugar and thyme. Cook 1 to 2 minutes, stirring occasionally, until sugar is dissolved. Remove from heat.

3 Unroll dough on cookie sheet. Starting at center, roll or press into 15x10-inch rectangle. Sprinkle cheese down center third of dough. Spoon onion mixture evenly over cheese.

4 With scissors or sharp knife, make cuts 1 inch apart on both long sides of dough to within ½ inch of filling. Alternately cross strips diagonally over filling; turn ends under and press to seal. Brush egg white over top. Sprinkle with poppy seed.

5 Bake 11 to 15 minutes or until crust is golden brown. Cool 5 minutes. Remove from cookie sheet; cut crosswise into slices.

1 Slice: Calories 150; Total Fat 7g (Saturated Fat 4g, Trans Fat 0g); Cholesterol 15mg; Sodium 310mg; Total Carbohydrate 18g (Dietary Fiber 0g); Protein 5g **Exchanges:** 1 Starch, 1½ Fat **Carbohydrate Choices:** 1

BUTTERNUT SQUASH BRUNCH BRAID

PREP TIME: 35 Minutes | **START TO FINISH:** 1 Hour 20 Minutes | 6 slices

2½ cups cubed (½ inch) seeded peeled butternut squash

1 tablespoon packed brown sugar

1 tablespoon extra-virgin olive oil

¼ teaspoon ground black pepper

4 slices bacon, chopped (about 4 oz)

1 medium onion, chopped

½ teaspoon ground thyme

1 can Pillsbury refrigerated crescent dough sheet

2 tablespoons grated Parmesan cheese

1 egg white, beaten

1 Heat oven to 425°F. In medium bowl, combine squash, brown sugar, olive oil and pepper; toss to coat. Spoon mixture into ungreased 15x10-inch pan with sides.

2 Bake 15 to 20 minutes, turning occasionally, or until squash is light brown on edges and tender when pierced with fork. Set aside. Reduce oven temperature to 375°F.

3 Meanwhile, in 10-inch skillet, cook bacon over medium heat until almost crisp. Using slotted spoon, transfer bacon pieces to paper towels. Add onion and thyme to bacon drippings in skillet. Cook and stir onion over medium heat until onion is brown and softened, about 3 minutes. Remove from heat; stir in bacon.

4 Spray large cookie sheet with cooking spray. Unroll dough onto cookie sheet. Starting at center, press into 12x8-inch rectangle. Spoon onion mixture in 4-inch-wide strip lengthwise down center of dough. Top onion with squash; sprinkle with cheese.

5 With scissors or sharp knife, make cuts 1 inch apart on long sides of dough to within ½ inch of filling. Alternately cross strips over filling; press ends to seal. Brush egg white over top.

6 Bake 20 to 25 minutes or until crust is deep golden brown. Cool 5 minutes. Remove from cookie sheet; cut crosswise into slices.

1 Slice: Calories 230; Total Fat 11g (Saturated Fat 4g, Trans Fat 0g); Cholesterol 5mg; Sodium 470mg; Total Carbohydrate 26g (Dietary Fiber 1g); Protein 6g **Exchanges:** 1½ Starch, ½ Vegetable, 2 Fat **Carbohydrate Choices:** 2

SERVE IT UP

◆ This savory bread is terrific served with roasted meat or poultry or with soups or stews.

CRESCENT ROLL HACKS

Try one of these clever crescent roll ideas with a container of crescent rolls!

CRESCENT CORN DOGS *(bottom)*

Press one side of dough triangles into corn meal. Roll up hot dogs in triangles. Bake on ungreased cookie sheet at 375°F 12 to 15 minutes.

EASY DOUGHNUTS *(left)*

Firmly press perforations in dough to seal. Cut rectangle in half; stack one half on top of the other. Cut 2 doughnuts and holes from dough; reroll to cut third doughnut. Fry in oil at 350°F 2 to 3 minutes per side. Let cool 5 minutes. Roll in cinnamon-sugar.

PIZZA ROLLS *(top)*

Spread a little pizza sauce on dough triangles. Top wide side of triangles with a few slices of pepperoni and a small piece of cheese. Roll up and bake on ungreased cookie sheet at 375°F 10 to 14 minutes. Serve with additional pizza sauce.

MAIN DISHES

BARBECUE CHICKEN PIZZAS

PREP TIME: 15 Minutes | **START TO FINISH:** 30 Minutes | **8 pizzas**

1 can Pillsbury Grands! Flaky Layers Original refrigerated biscuits (8 biscuits)

2 cups shredded or diced cooked chicken

1 cup barbecue sauce

1 cup shredded Colby–Monterey Jack cheese blend (4 oz)

1 Heat oven to 375°F. Spray 2 large or 3 small cookie sheets with cooking spray.

2 Separate dough into 8 biscuits; press each biscuit into 6-inch round. In medium bowl, mix chicken and barbecue sauce. Top each round with ¼ cup chicken mixture; sprinkle with 2 tablespoons cheese. Place biscuits on cookie sheets.

3 Bake 10 to 15 minutes or until crust is golden brown and cheese is bubbly.

1 Pizza: Calories 340; Total Fat 14g (Saturated Fat 5g, Trans Fat 3.5g); Cholesterol 45mg; Sodium 1020mg; Total Carbohydrate 38g (Dietary Fiber 0g); Protein 16g **Exchanges:** 1½ Starch, 1 Other Carbohydrate, ½ Lean Meat, ½ Medium-Fat Meat, ½ High-Fat Meat, 1 Fat **Carbohydrate Choices:** 2½

KITCHEN SECRET

◆ Use any flavor barbecue sauce or cheese that you have on hand for these pizzas.

KITCHEN HACK

NO DRIPS

Avoid frequent cleanups in your refrigerator by placing raw meats on trays with sides or in containers.

CRESCENT MUMMY PIZZAS

PREP TIME: 15 Minutes | **START TO FINISH:** 30 Minutes | 8 pizzas

1   can Pillsbury refrigerated crescent dough sheet

⅓   cup pizza sauce

8   slices mozzarella cheese (from 8-oz package), cut into 8 strips each

16   ripe olive slices or mini pepperoni slices

1   Heat oven to 375°F. Spray large cookie sheet with cooking spray.

2   Unroll dough on cutting board; cut into 4 rectangles. Using pizza cutter or sharp knife, cut each rectangle crosswise in half to make 8 squares. Place squares on cookie sheet, and press out slightly.

3   Bake 8 to 9 minutes or until light golden brown; remove from oven.

4   Spread about 2 teaspoons of the pizza sauce on top of each square. Arrange 8 strips of cheese over sauce, alternating and overlapping strips to look like mummy bandages. Place 2 olive or pepperoni slices on cheese for eyes.

5   Bake 2 to 3 minutes longer or until cheese slightly melts. Serve warm.

1 Pizza: Calories 190; Total Fat 11g (Saturated Fat 5g, Trans Fat 0g); Cholesterol 20mg; Sodium 430mg; Total Carbohydrate 15g (Dietary Fiber 0g); Protein 9g **Exchanges:** 1 Starch, 1 Medium-Fat Meat, 1 Fat **Carbohydrate Choices:** 1

KITCHEN SECRETS

◆ Up the flavor of these pizzas by adding chopped Canadian bacon or pepperoni before adding the cheese.

◆ If you prefer, you can use 1 can Pillsbury refrigerated crescent dinner rolls (8 rolls) instead of the dough sheet. Unroll rolls, separate into 4 rectangles and firmly press perforations to seal. Continue as directed.

ADD A GARNISH

◆ Serve with extra pizza sauce for dipping if you like.

POTATO SAUSAGE UPSIDE-DOWN PIZZA

PREP TIME: 25 Minutes | **START TO FINISH:** 1 Hour 30 Minutes | **6 servings**

1 lb bulk spicy pork sausage

2 cups thinly sliced baby red potatoes (about ⅓ lb)

1 tablespoon olive oil

2 large onions, halved, thinly sliced (2 cups)

4 cups baby arugula and spinach blend (from 5-oz container), chopped

2 teaspoons chopped fresh rosemary

2 cups shredded Italian cheese blend (8 oz)

1 can Pillsbury refrigerated classic pizza crust

1 Heat oven to 375°F. In 12-inch nonstick skillet, cook sausage over medium-high heat, stirring occasionally, 5 to 8 minutes or until no longer pink; drain. Add potatoes; cook, stirring occasionally, 3 to 4 minutes or until potatoes are crisp-tender. Using slotted spoon, transfer mixture to 13x9-inch (3-quart) ungreased glass baking dish.

2 In same skillet, heat oil over medium heat until hot. Add onions; cook 12 to 18 minutes, stirring frequently or until golden brown. Remove from heat. Stir in greens and 1 teaspoon of the rosemary. Spoon evenly over sausage mixture. Sprinkle evenly with 1 cup of the cheese.

3 Unroll dough over cheese, gently stretching to sides of baking dish. Fold edges under. Sprinkle with remaining 1 cup cheese; sprinkle with remaining 1 teaspoon rosemary.

4 Bake 20 to 25 minutes or until crust is golden brown. Cut into 3 rows by 2 rows.

1 Serving: Calories 490; Total Fat 23g (Saturated Fat 10g, Trans Fat 0g); Cholesterol 65mg; Sodium 950mg; Total Carbohydrate 47g (Dietary Fiber 2g); Protein 22g **Exchanges:** 1 Starch, 2 Other Carbohydrate, 1 Vegetable, 2½ High-Fat Meat, ½ Fat **Carbohydrate Choices:** 3

KITCHEN SECRETS

◆ Any type of baby potatoes can be used in this pizza. Use what you have on hand or what's on sale at your grocery store.

◆ Try fresh thyme instead of the rosemary.

SERVE IT UP

◆ Pair this pizza with a simple green salad for a satisfying dinner.

PIZZA CUPCAKES

PREP TIME: 15 Minutes | **START TO FINISH:** 30 Minutes | 8 cupcakes

1   can Pillsbury refrigerated crescent dinner rolls (8 rolls)

½   cup pizza sauce

¼   cup mini pepperoni slices (from 5-oz package)

¼   lb mild Italian sausage, cooked. drained

½   cup shredded mozzarella cheese (2 oz)

1   Heat oven to 375°F. Spray 8 regular-size muffin cups with cooking spray. Unroll dough; separate into 8 triangles. Press 1 triangle on bottom and up side of each muffin cup.

2   In small bowl, mix sauce, pepperoni, sausage and ¼ cup of the cheese. Spoon about 2 tablespoons mixture into each dough-lined cup; sprinkle each with about 1 teaspoon cheese.

3   Bake 16 to 18 minutes or until lightly browned. Immediately remove from cups and serve.

1 Cupcake: Calories 190; Total Fat 12g (Saturated Fat 4.5g, Trans Fat 1.5g); Cholesterol 15mg; Sodium 480mg; Total Carbohydrate 13g (Dietary Fiber 0g); Protein 7g **Exchanges:** 1 Starch, ½ High-Fat Meat, 1½ Fat **Carbohydrate Choices:** 1

KITCHEN SECRET

◆ If you can't find mini pepperoni slices, purchase larger ones, and cut them into fourths to fit in the muffin cups.

KITCHEN HACK

KEEP A STASH

Cook up an extra pound of ground beef or pork sausage while cooking one for a recipe to keep on hand for easy dinner prep. Drain cooked meat in a colander or on paper towels. Store tightly covered in the refrigerator up to 3 days or freeze up to 2 months.

BREAKFAST QUICHES TO GO

PREP TIME: 25 Minutes | START TO FINISH: 45 Minutes | 16 quiches

2 cans Pillsbury refrigerated crescent dinner rolls (8 rolls each)

1 package (8 oz) cream cheese, softened

3 eggs

1 small onion, chopped (¼ cup)

1 box (9 oz) frozen chopped spinach, thawed, squeezed to drain

¼ teaspoon salt

⅛ teaspoon pepper

1 cup shredded mozzarella cheese (4 oz)

1   Heat oven to 350°F. Spray 16 regular-size muffin cups with cooking spray.

2   Unroll both cans of dough; separate each into 8 triangles. Press 1 triangle on bottom and up side of each muffin cup.

3   In medium bowl, beat cream cheese with electric mixer on medium speed until smooth. Add eggs, one at a time, beating well after each addition. Stir in onion, spinach, salt and pepper until well mixed. Fold in cheese. Divide mixture evenly among muffin cups (fill just to top—do not overfill).

4   Bake 15 to 20 minutes or until knife inserted in center comes out clean and edges are golden brown. Remove from pan. Serve warm.

1 Quiche: Calories 190; Total Fat 12g (Saturated Fat 6g, Trans Fat 0g); Cholesterol 55mg; Sodium 360mg; Total Carbohydrate 14g (Dietary Fiber 0g); Protein 6g **Exchanges:** 1 Starch, ½ Medium-Fat Meat, 2 Fat **Carbohydrate Choices:** 1

KITCHEN SECRET

◆ You can make these quiches ahead and reheat when ready. Prepare and bake as directed. Cool quiches completely. Wrap tightly in plastic wrap and freeze up to 3 months. Thaw in refrigerator overnight. Unwrap; microwave 1 quiche on High about 1 minute or until hot.

KITCHEN HACK

HEARTY NAPKINS

Pick up some inexpensive wash cloths to use as hearty napkins for messy meals such as sloppy joes or ribs. Then throw them in the wash so they'll be ready to use again.

PEPPERONI PIZZA BAKE

PREP TIME: 10 Minutes | **START TO FINISH:** 35 Minutes | **6 servings**

1 can Pillsbury Grands! Flaky Layers Original refrigerated biscuits (8 biscuits)

1 can (8 oz) pizza sauce

2 cups finely shredded mozzarella cheese (8 oz)

16 slices (1½ inch) pepperoni

1 Heat oven to 375°F. Spray 13x9-inch (3-quart) baking dish with cooking spray.

2 Separate dough into 8 biscuits; cut each into 8 pieces. In large bowl, toss biscuit pieces, pizza sauce and 1 cup of the cheese. Spoon into dish; top with pepperoni and remaining 1 cup cheese.

3 Bake 20 to 23 minutes or until biscuits are golden brown and no longer doughy in center of pan.

1 Serving: Calories 390; Total Fat 18g (Saturated Fat 9g, Trans Fat 0g); Cholesterol 30mg; Sodium 1070mg; Total Carbohydrate 40g (Dietary Fiber 1g); Protein 16g **Exchanges:** 2 Starch, ½ Other Carbohydrate, 1½ Medium-Fat Meat, 2 Fat **Carbohydrate Choices:** 2½

KITCHEN HACK

NO SLIP

Put a damp towel under your cutting board to keep it from sliding when cutting or chopping.

SHEET-PAN HAM AND APPLE GRILLED CHEESE

PREP TIME: 15 Minutes | **START TO FINISH:** 45 Minutes | **12 sandwiches**

1 tablespoon butter, melted

2 cans (8 oz each) Pillsbury refrigerated crescent dough sheet

2 cups shredded Cheddar cheese (8 oz)

¼ lb thinly sliced cooked ham

1 apple, thinly sliced

1 ripe avocado, peeled, thinly sliced

1 teaspoon garlic-pepper blend

1 Heat oven to 375°F. In 15x10x1-inch pan, brush 12 x 8-inch area with half of the melted butter. Unroll 1 can of dough; press onto melted butter.

2 Sprinkle 1 cup of the cheese over dough to within ½ inch from edges. Top with ham, apple, avocado and remaining cheese. Sprinkle with ¼ teaspoon of the garlic-pepper blend. Unroll remaining can of dough; place over cheese, gently stretching to cover filling. Press edges to seal. Brush with remaining melted butter; sprinkle with remaining garlic-pepper blend.

3 Bake 20 to 25 minutes or until deep golden brown. Let stand 10 minutes. Cut into 3 rows by 2 rows; cut each rectangle diagonally to form 2 triangles.

1 Sandwich: Calories 240; Total Fat 14g (Saturated Fat 6g, Trans Fat 0g); Cholesterol 25mg; Sodium 550mg; Total Carbohydrate 22g (Dietary Fiber 1g); Protein 8g **Exchanges:** 1 Starch, ½ Other Carbohydrate, ½ High-Fat Meat, 2 Fat **Carbohydrate Choices:** 1½

KITCHEN SECRETS

◆ Feel free to use your favorite type of easy-melting cheese in this sandwich. American, Swiss, mozzarella and Italian cheese blend are all good options.

◆ You can use 2 cans Pillsbury refrigerated crescent dinner rolls (8 rolls each) for the dough sheets. Unroll dough and firmly press perforations to seal. Continue as directed.

Top to bottom:
Sheet-Pan Ham and Apple Grilled Cheese (above)
Sheet-Pan Grilled Pimiento Cheese and Bacon (page 156)
Sheet-Pan Grilled Cheese with Sausage and Mashed Potatoes (page 157)

KITCHEN HACK

SIMPLE SHOPPING

Keep a running shopping list inside your cupboard door or on your phone, noting items that are running low or get used up. When you go to the store, it's easy to know what you need.

SHEET-PAN GRILLED PIMIENTO CHEESE AND BACON

PREP TIME: 20 Minutes | **START TO FINISH:** 55 Minutes | **12 sandwiches**

1   tablespoon butter, melted

2   cans (8 oz each) Pillsbury refrigerated crescent dough sheet

1   cup pimiento cheese (from 10-oz container)

2   tablespoons chopped pickled sliced jalapeño chiles (from 16-oz jar), drained

1   cup shredded sharp Cheddar cheese (4 oz)

6   slices bacon, crisply cooked, chopped

1   tablespoon sesame seed

1   Heat oven to 375°F. In 15x10x1-inch pan, brush a 12x8-inch rectangle with half of the melted butter. Unroll 1 can of the dough; press onto melted butter in pan.

2   In small bowl, mix pimiento cheese and chiles until well blended. Spread evenly over dough. Sprinkle with Cheddar cheese and bacon.

3   Unroll remaining can of dough; place over cheese, gently stretching to cover filling. Press edges to seal. Brush with remaining butter; sprinkle with sesame seed.

4   Bake 20 to 25 minutes or until deep golden brown. Let stand 10 minutes. Cut into 3 rows by 2 rows; cut each rectangle diagonally into 2 triangles.

1 Sandwich: Calories 230; Total Fat 14g (Saturated Fat 7g, Trans Fat 0g); Cholesterol 30mg; Sodium 560mg; Total Carbohydrate 21g (Dietary Fiber 0g); Protein 7g **Exchanges:** 1 Starch, ½ Other Carbohydrate, ½ High-Fat Meat, 2 Fat **Carbohydrate Choices:** 1½

KITCHEN SECRETS

◆ You can find pimiento cheese in the deli section of your favorite grocery store. We've added chopped pickled jalapeños to the pimiento cheese in this recipe. If your pimiento cheese already contains jalapeños, omit adding the ones called for in this recipe.

◆ It's best to use deli pimiento cheese for the success of this recipe, rather than the jarred variety.

ADD A GARNISH

◆ To jazz up these grilled cheese sandwiches, spear jalapeño slices and grape tomatoes on toothpicks to poke into the sandwiches just before serving.

SHEET-PAN GRILLED CHEESE WITH SAUSAGE AND MASHED POTATOES

PREP TIME: 15 Minutes | **START TO FINISH:** 50 Minutes | 12 sandwiches

1   tablespoon butter, melted

2   cans (8 oz each) Pillsbury refrigerated crescent dough sheet

½   lb bulk Italian sausage

1   cup mashed potatoes

½   cup sour cream

¾   cup chopped green onions with tops

8   slices Cheddar cheese (about 1 oz each)

1. Heat oven to 375°F. In 15x10x1-inch pan, brush a 12x8-inch rectangle with half of the melted butter. Unroll 1 can of the dough; press onto melted butter in pan.

2. In 10-inch skillet, cook sausage over medium heat 5 to 6 minutes, stirring frequently, until browned. Remove from heat; drain well. Stir in mashed potatoes, sour cream and ½ cup of the green onions.

3. Spread potato mixture onto dough to within ½ inch of edges. Arrange cheese evenly over potato mixture. Unroll remaining can of dough; place over layered ingredients, gently stretching to cover filling. Press edges to seal. Brush with remaining melted butter; sprinkle with remaining ¼ cup green onions, pressing lightly into dough.

4. Bake 20 to 25 minutes or until deep golden brown. Let stand 10 minutes. Cut into 3 rows by 2 rows; cut each rectangle diagonally into 2 triangles.

1 Sandwich: Calories 290; Total Fat 18g (Saturated Fat 8g, Trans Fat 0g); Cholesterol 35mg; Sodium 560mg; Total Carbohydrate 23g (Dietary Fiber 0g); Protein 9g **Exchanges:** 1 Starch, ½ Other Carbohydrate, 1 High-Fat Meat, 2 Fat **Carbohydrate Choices:** 1½

KITCHEN SECRET

◆ You can use hot or mild Italian sausage in this recipe depending on your family's preference. If bulk sausage isn't available, remove the casings from sausage links before browning.

ADD A GARNISH

◆ Serve with additional sour cream and green onion if you like.

SAVORY HAM WAFFLE SANDWICHES

PREP TIME: 20 Minutes | **START TO FINISH:** 20 Minutes | **5 sandwiches**

1 can Pillsbury Grands! Juniors Flaky Layers refrigerated biscuits (10 biscuits)

10 slices (⅔ oz each) Muenster cheese

2½ teaspoons sweet honey mustard

5 oz very thinly sliced cooked ham (from deli)

1. Heat Belgian or regular waffle maker according to manufacturer's directions. Separate dough into 10 biscuits. Press or roll each into 4½-inch round.

2. Depending on size of waffle maker, place 1 or 2 biscuit rounds at a time in hot waffle maker. Bake about 2 minutes or until golden brown. Remove to cooling rack. Immediately place 1 slice cheese on each hot waffle. Spread ½ teaspoon mustard over cheese on each of 5 waffles.

3. Divide ham evenly among the 5 cheese- and mustard-topped waffles; top each with another waffle, cheese side down. Serve warm.

1 Sandwich: Calories 390; Total Fat 21g (Saturated Fat 11g, Trans Fat 0g); Cholesterol 50mg; Sodium 1330mg; Total Carbohydrate 31g (Dietary Fiber 0g); Protein 19g **Exchanges:** 1½ Starch, ½ Other Carbohydrate, 1 Very Lean Meat, 1 High-Fat Meat, 2½ Fat **Carbohydrate Choices:** 2

KITCHEN SECRETS

◆ Ask at your deli for honey-roasted or honey-baked ham to add another level of sweetness to these sandwiches!

◆ Omit the sweet honey mustard, and drizzle a bit of warm honey over the ham instead.

KITCHEN HACK

EASY SKIMMING

Remove fat easily from soups and stews by allowing the food to cool in the refrigerator about 30 minutes. The fat will rise to the top and solidify, making it easy to skim off and discard.

BREAKFAST BISCUIT BUNS

PREP TIME: 20 Minutes | **START TO FINISH:** 50 Minutes | 8 buns

1   lb pepper bacon

½   cup finely chopped onion

1   can Pillsbury Grands!
    Flaky Layers refrigerated
    buttermilk biscuits
    (8 biscuits)

8   eggs

½   cup shredded smoked
    Cheddar cheese (2 oz)

    Pepper, if desired

1   Heat oven to 350°F. In 10-inch skillet, cook bacon over medium-high heat 10 to 12 minutes or until bacon is crisp. Remove from pan to paper towels, and crumble. Remove all but 1 tablespoon bacon drippings from skillet. Add onion to skillet; cook and stir about 2 minutes or until onion is tender. In small bowl, mix onion and bacon. Set aside.

2   Spray 8 jumbo muffin cups or 8 (6-oz) custard cups with cooking spray. Separate dough into 8 biscuits. Place 1 biscuit in each muffin cup, pressing dough three-fourths of the way up side of cup. Divide bacon mixture evenly among biscuit cups; crack 1 egg over each. Top each with 1 tablespoon cheese and sprinkle with pepper.

3   Bake 22 to 26 minutes or until egg whites and yolks are firm but not runny. Run small knife around cups to loosen. Serve immediately.

1 Bun: Calories 380; Total Fat 22g (Saturated Fat 9g, Trans Fat 0g); Cholesterol 210mg; Sodium 1030mg; Total Carbohydrate 27g (Dietary Fiber 0g); Protein 17g **Exchanges:** 1 Starch, 1 Other Carbohydrate, 1 Medium-Fat Meat, 1 High-Fat Meat, 1½ Fat **Carbohydrate Choices:** 2

KITCHEN SECRETS

◆ Make a batch of these ahead to have ready when you are! Remove baked buns from pan to cooling rack. When cool, place buns on dinner plate; cover and refrigerate up to 1 week. Reheat buns uncovered on cookie sheet at 350°F about 5 minutes or until hot.

◆ Smoked Gouda can be used instead of smoked Cheddar. Or if you prefer a cheese without a smoky flavor, substitute regular Cheddar, Gouda or Swiss.

◆ To reduce the sodium, use only ¾ pound of bacon, or look for lower sodium bacon.

BACON-EGG BREAKFAST BITES

PREP TIME: 20 Minutes | **START TO FINISH:** 40 Minutes | **12 breakfast bites**

12 slices precooked bacon (from 2.1-oz package)

1 can Pillsbury Place 'N Bake refrigerated crescent rounds (8 rounds)

24 frozen potato nuggets (from 2-lb bag)

5 eggs

¼ teaspoon salt

¼ teaspoon ground black pepper

1 Heat oven to 350°F. Generously spray 24 mini muffin cups with cooking spray.

2 Cut each bacon slice crosswise in half. Separate dough into 8 rounds. Unroll 1 round; cut crosswise into thirds, forming strips of dough. Place 1 slice bacon on 1 dough strip. Top with 1 potato nugget and roll up, stretching dough and pinching ends to seal. Place in mini muffin cup spiral side up. Repeat with remaining rounds, bacon and potato nuggets.

3 In medium bowl, beat eggs, salt and pepper until well blended. Very carefully spoon 1 scant tablespoon egg mixture around each dough-wrapped potato nugget.

4 Bake 13 to 20 minutes or until light brown and egg mixture is set. Remove from muffin cups to serving platter. Serve warm.

1 Serving (2 Breakfast Bites): Calories 180; Total Fat 11g (Saturated Fat 3.5g, Trans Fat 1.5g); Cholesterol 95mg; Sodium 440mg; Total Carbohydrate 12g (Dietary Fiber 0g); Protein 7g **Exchanges:** 1 Starch, ½ Medium-Fat Meat, 1½ Fat **Carbohydrate Choices:** 1

KITCHEN SECRET

◆ You can substitute 1 can Pillsbury refrigerated crescent dough sheet for the crescent dough rounds. Unroll dough; cut into 6 rows by 4 rows. Continue as directed.

ADD A GARNISH

◆ After removing the bites from the oven, garnish with chopped fresh parsley for a splash of color.

HAM AND MUSHROOM BREAKFAST TARTS

PREP TIME: 25 Minutes | START TO FINISH: 45 Minutes | 4 tarts

1   can Pillsbury refrigerated crescent dough sheet

1   tablespoon butter

¾   cup coarsely chopped fresh mushrooms

½   cup chopped green onions with tops

½   cup shredded Swiss cheese (2 oz)

½   cup diced ham

4   eggs

½   teaspoon dried thyme

    Pepper, if desired

1. Heat oven to 375°F. Line large cookie sheet with cooking parchment paper. Unroll dough on cutting board. Press or roll to form 15x10-inch rectangle. Cut into 4 rectangles (7½ x 5 inches). Place rectangles on cookie sheet. Fold sides of each rectangle over to create a "lip" on each side.

2. In 1-quart saucepan, heat butter over medium heat until melted. Add mushrooms and onions; cook 2 to 3 minutes or until vegetables are softened. Spoon 2 tablespoons of the Swiss cheese, 2 tablespoons of the ham and 2 tablespoons of the vegetable mixture onto each rectangle, leaving room in the center for each egg. Break 1 egg in center of each rectangle; sprinkle with thyme and pepper. (Egg white may run over slightly onto cookie sheet.)

3. Bake 18 to 22 minutes or until edges of dough are golden and egg whites and yolks are firm, not runny.

1 Tart: Calories 370; Total Fat 20g (Saturated Fat 9g, Trans Fat 0g); Cholesterol 215mg; Sodium 810mg; Total Carbohydrate 29g (Dietary Fiber 0g); Protein 17g **Exchanges:** 1 Starch, ½ Other Carbohydrate, ½ Vegetable, 2 Medium-Fat Meat, 2 Fat **Carbohydrate Choices:** 2

KITCHEN SECRETS

◆ Using fresh eggs will reduce the chance of runny whites and help the whole egg stay in the center of the dough rectangle.

◆ You can use any type of cheese on these tarts: Cheddar, mozzarella, and goat cheese are all good choices.

KITCHEN HACK

CUTTING RAW MEAT

It's easier to thinly slice raw meat if you partially freeze it first. Thirty to 60 minutes should be enough to make it firm but not frozen—perfect for slicing.

BBQ CHICKEN CRESCENT POCKETS

PREP TIME: 15 Minutes | **START TO FINISH:** 30 Minutes | **4 pockets**

1 package (16 oz) barbecue sauce with hickory-smoked pulled chicken

½ cup shredded Monterey Jack cheese (2 oz)

1 can Pillsbury refrigerated crescent dough sheet

1 Heat oven to 375°F. Cut chicken into smaller pieces. In medium bowl, mix chicken mixture and cheese.

2 Unroll dough on cutting board; cut into 4 rectangles. Place rectangles on ungreased cookie sheet. Onto the short-side half of each rectangle, spoon about ½ cup chicken mixture. Fold untopped dough over filling, firmly pressing edges with fork to seal. With fork, prick top to allow steam to escape. Repeat for remaining rectangles and filling.

3 Bake 13 to 15 minutes or until deep golden brown. Serve warm.

1 Pocket: Calories 400; Total Fat 16g (Saturated Fat 6g, Trans Fat 0g); Cholesterol 70mg; Sodium 820mg; Total Carbohydrate 38g (Dietary Fiber 0g); Protein 26g **Exchanges:** 2½ Starch, 2 Very Lean Meat, ½ High-Fat Meat, 2 Fat **Carbohydrate Choices:** 2½

KITCHEN SECRET

◆ You can substitute 1 can Pillsbury refrigerated crescent dinner rolls (8 rolls) for the dough sheet. Press diagonal perforations to seal and separate into 4 rectangles.

SERVE IT UP

◆ Serve with a side of corn on the cob and coleslaw.

ADD A GARNISH

◆ Top pockets with chopped fresh cilantro leaves or sliced green onions before baking.

MONTE CRISTO MELTS

PREP TIME: 20 Minutes | **START TO FINISH:** 35 Minutes | 8 sandwiches

1½ cups shredded Gouda cheese (6 oz)

1¼ cups finely chopped cooked ham (about 6 oz)

⅓ cup mayonnaise or salad dressing

1 box Pillsbury refrigerated pie crusts, softened as directed on box

1 egg yolk

1 teaspoon water

½ teaspoon smoked paprika

1. Heat oven to 425°F. In medium bowl, stir together cheese, ham and mayonnaise; set aside.

2. On lightly floured work surface, roll each pie crust into 14-inch round. Using 6-inch round plate, cut 3 rounds from each crust. Reroll remaining dough, and cut 2 more 6-inch rounds. Spoon about ¼ cup cheese mixture onto half of each round to within ¼ inch from edge. Moisten edge of each round with water. Fold untopped dough over filling; press edges with fork to seal. Place sandwiches about 2 inches apart on 2 ungreased large cookie sheets.

3. Beat egg yolk, water and paprika with fork. Brush top of each sandwich with egg mixture; cut small slit in top to allow steam to escape.

4. Bake 12 to 16 minutes or until golden brown. Serve warm.

1 Sandwich: Calories 370; Total Fat 25g (Saturated Fat 10g, Trans Fat 0g); Cholesterol 70mg; Sodium 740mg; Total Carbohydrate 23g (Dietary Fiber 0g); Protein 11g **Exchanges:** ½ Starch, 1 Other Carbohydrate, 1½ Medium-Fat Meat, 3½ Fat **Carbohydrate Choices:** 1½

SERVE IT UP

◆ Serve these sandwiches with a lightly dressed tossed salad and a wedge of cantaloupe.

ADD A GARNISH

◆ In true Monte Cristo tradition, serve these melts with blackberry preserves and a dusting of powdered sugar.

KITCHEN HACK

EASY SHREDDING

Soft cheese is easier to shred when placed in the freezer for 15 minutes first.

SPICY GRILLED BISCUIT BURGERS

PREP TIME: 30 Minutes | **START TO FINISH:** 30 Minutes | 8 burgers

2	lb lean (at least 80%) ground beef
¼	cup pickled jalapeño slices, drained, finely chopped
8	slices (1 oz each) pepper Jack cheese, each cut in half
1	can Pillsbury Grands Flaky Layers Original refrigerated (8 biscuits)
	Cooking spray
½	cup chipotle mayonnaise

1 Heat gas or charcoal grill. In medium bowl, mix ground beef and 2 tablespoons of the jalapeños. Shape mixture into 8 patties.

2 Place patties on grill over medium heat. Cover grill; cook 10 to 12 minutes, turning once, until meat thermometer inserted in center of patties reads 160°F. Place cheese slices on patties and cook about 1 minute longer or until cheese melts. Remove burgers from grill; cover and keep warm. Reduce heat on grill to low.

3 Separate dough into 8 biscuits. Spray both sides of each biscuit with cooking spray. Place biscuits on grill over low heat. Cook, uncovered, about 4 minutes or until light golden brown; turn. Cover grill; cook 2 to 3 minutes longer or until golden brown.

4 Split each biscuit in half. Place burger on bottom half. Top each burger with mayonnaise, some of the remaining jalapeños and biscuit top.

1 Burger: Calories 570; Total Fat 38g (Saturated Fat 13g, Trans Fat 4.5g); Cholesterol 105mg; Sodium 960mg; Total Carbohydrate 26g (Dietary Fiber 0g); Protein 29g **Exchanges:** 1½ Starch, 3½ Lean Meat, 5½ Fat **Carbohydrate Choices:** 2

KITCHEN HACK

SQUIRREL IT AWAY

If you're lucky enough to have leftovers, save them for an easy and inexpensive lunch the next day. Store them in microwavable storage containers and reheat just until hot.

BARBECUE CRESCENT DOGS

PREP TIME: 10 Minutes | **START TO FINISH:** 25 Minutes | **8 crescent dogs**

8   hot dogs

¼   cup pickle relish

1   can Pillsbury refrigerated crescent dinner rolls (8 rolls)

½   cup refrigerated original barbecue sauce with shredded pork (from 18-oz container)

2   medium green onions, sliced (2 tablespoons)

1   Heat oven to 375°F. Slit each hot dog lengthwise to within ½ inch of ends. Insert ½ tablespoon pickle relish into each slit.

2   Unroll dough; separate into 8 triangles. Spread 1 tablespoon barbecue sauce with pork on each triangle. Wrap 1 dough triangle around each hot dog. Place on ungreased cookie sheet, stuffed side up.

3   Bake 14 to 15 minutes or until golden brown. Sprinkle with green onion.

1 Crescent Dog: Calories 280; Total Fat 19g (Saturated Fat 7g, Trans Fat 0g); Cholesterol 30mg; Sodium 880mg; Total Carbohydrate 18g (Dietary Fiber 0g); Protein 7g **Exchanges:** 1 Other Carbohydrate, 1 High-Fat Meat, 2½ Fat **Carbohydrate Choices:** 1

KITCHEN SECRET

◆ Top the hot dogs with yellow or brown mustard before sprinkling with the onions. You can also swap ketchup for the green onions if you like.

BACON-CHEESEBURGER CALZONES

PREP TIME: 30 Minutes | **START TO FINISH:** 50 Minutes | **8 calzones**

4 slices bacon, cut into ¼ inch pieces

1 lb lean (at least 80%) ground beef

¼ cup dried instant minced onion

¼ cup chopped hamburger pickle slices

¼ cup ranch dressing

2 cans Pillsbury refrigerated crescent dinner rolls (8 rolls each)

2 Italian plum (Roma) tomatoes, thinly sliced

4 slices (¾ oz each) American or Cheddar cheese, each cut in half

1 egg, beaten

1. Heat oven to 375°F. In 10-inch nonstick skillet, cook bacon over medium heat 2 minutes. Add ground beef and onion; cook, stirring occasionally, until beef is thoroughly cooked; drain if necessary. Stir in pickles and dressing.

2. Unroll both cans of dough; separate each into 4 rectangles. Place on ungreased cookie sheet. Press each into 7x4-inch rectangle, firmly pressing perforations to seal.

3. Onto the short-side half of each rectangle, spoon about ⅓ cup ground beef mixture. Top with tomato slices and 1 piece cheese. Fold untopped dough over filling; press edges with fork to seal (sandwiches will be full). Brush top with egg.

4. Bake 15 to 20 minutes or until deep golden brown. Immediately remove from cookie sheet and cut in half crosswise, if desired. Serve warm.

1 Calzone: Calories 420; Total Fat 28g (Saturated Fat 11g, Trans Fat 0.5g); Cholesterol 75mg; Sodium 820mg; Total Carbohydrate 25g (Dietary Fiber 0g); Protein 16g **Exchanges:** 1 Starch, ½ Other Carbohydrate, 2 Lean Meat, 4½ Fat **Carbohydrate Choices:** 1½

KITCHEN SECRET

◆ Bacon grease can be messy. For easy cleanup, carefully pour it into a "bowl" made of foil, then fold in the edges and toss once the grease has cooled.

BEEF AND BEAN CRESCENT BURRITOS

PREP TIME: 10 Minutes | **START TO FINISH:** 30 Minutes | 8 burritos

½ lb ground beef, cooked, drained

½ cup black beans (from 15-oz can), rinsed, drained

2 tablespoons taco seasoning mix (from 1-oz package)

3 tablespoons water

2 cans Pillsbury refrigerated crescent dough sheet (1 sheet each)

1 cup shredded Cheddar cheese (4 oz)

1. Heat oven to 375°F. In 10-inch skillet, mix beef, beans, taco seasoning mix and water. Heat to boiling over medium-high heat, stirring occasionally.

2. Unroll dough onto cutting board; cut into 8 rectangles. Divide beef mixture evenly among rectangles, spooning down center of each rectangle. Sprinkle with ½ cup of the cheese. Starting with short side, roll up each rectangle; pinch edge to seal. Place seam side down on ungreased cookie sheet. Sprinkle with remaining cheese.

3. Bake 15 to 20 minutes or until golden brown.

1 Burrito: Calories 300; Total Fat 14g (Saturated Fat 6g, Trans Fat 0g); Cholesterol 30mg; Sodium 750mg; Total Carbohydrate 32g (Dietary Fiber 1g); Protein 12g **Exchanges:** 2 Starch, 1 Medium-Fat Meat, 1½ Fat **Carbohydrate Choices:** 2

KITCHEN SECRET

◆ You can use 2 cans Pillsbury refrigerated crescent dinner rolls (8 rolls each) instead of the dough sheets. Firmly press diagonal perforations to seal and separate into 8 rectangles.

EASY TACO MELTS

PREP TIME: 20 Minutes | **START TO FINISH:** 35 Minutes | 8 sandwiches

1 lb lean (at least 80%) ground beef

1 package (1 oz) taco seasoning mix

⅔ cup water

½ cup thick 'n chunky salsa

1 can Pillsbury Grands! Flaky Layers Original refrigerated biscuits (8 biscuits)

½ cup shredded Monterey Jack cheese or Mexican cheese blend (2 oz)

1 Heat oven to 375°F. Spray large cookie sheet with cooking spray.

2 In medium saucepan, cook beef over medium-high heat until thoroughly cooked; drain. Stir in taco seasoning mix, water and salsa. Cook, stirring occasionally, until thickened.

3 Separate dough into 8 biscuits; press each into 6-inch round. Spoon ⅓ cup meat mixture and 1 tablespoon cheese onto center of each round. Fold dough in half over filling; press edges to seal. Place on cookie sheet.

4 Bake 9 to 14 minutes or until golden brown.

1 Sandwich: Calories 310; Total Fat 15g (Saturated Fat 6g, Trans Fat 0g); Cholesterol 40mg; Sodium 870mg; Total Carbohydrate 29g (Dietary Fiber 1g); Protein 16g **Exchanges:** 1 Starch, 1 Other Carbohydrate, 2 Lean Meat, 1½ Fat **Carbohydrate Choices:** 2

SERVE IT UP

◆ To complete the menu, add a crisp green salad of romaine lettuce topped with fresh orange slices and drizzled with your favorite dressing.

ADD A GARNISH

◆ Serve these sandwiches with traditional taco fixin's—sour cream, guacamole and salsa.

EGGS BENEDICT BUBBLE-UP

PREP TIME: 10 Minutes | **START TO FINISH:** 50 Minutes | **8 servings**

1 can Pillsbury Grands! Flaky Layers refrigerated buttermilk biscuits (5 biscuits)

1 package (5 or 6 oz) Canadian bacon, cut into strips

8 eggs

2¼ cups milk

¼ teaspoon salt

¼ teaspoon pepper

¼ cup sliced green onions with tops

1 package (.9 oz) hollandaise sauce mix

¼ cup butter

1 Heat oven to 350°F. Spray 13x9-inch (3-quart) glass baking dish with cooking spray.

2 Separate dough into 5 biscuits; cut each into 8 pieces. Sprinkle pieces evenly in baking dish; top with Canadian bacon.

3 In large bowl, beat eggs, 1¼ cups of the milk, the salt and pepper with whisk until mixed well; stir in onions. Pour over Canadian bacon.

4 Bake 30 to 35 minutes or until knife inserted in center comes out clean and biscuits are deep golden brown.

5 Meanwhile, prepare hollandaise sauce as directed on package using remaining 1 cup milk and the butter; keep warm. Drizzle ½ cup of the hollandaise sauce over biscuits. Cover and refrigerate remaining sauce for another use. Let stand 5 minutes before serving.

1 Serving: Calories 370; Total Fat 19g (Saturated Fat 9g, Trans Fat 0g); Cholesterol 215mg; Sodium 900mg; Total Carbohydrate 33g (Dietary Fiber 0g); Protein 16g **Exchanges:** 1½ Starch, ½ Other Carbohydrate, ½ Lean Meat, 1 Medium-Fat Meat, 2½ Fat **Carbohydrate Choices:** 2

KITCHEN SECRET

◆ Leftover hollandaise sauce has many uses. Serve it with vegetables or over poached or scrambled eggs, stir it into deviled eggs or use it as a dipping sauce for crab cakes or cooked salmon.

ADD A GARNISH

◆ Garnish with additional thinly sliced green onions.

Clockwise from top:
Chicken-Veggie Ranch
Bubble-Up (page 183)
Chicken Taco
Bubble-Up (page 182)
Eggs Benedict
Bubble-Up (above)

CHICKEN TACO BUBBLE-UP

PREP TIME: 20 Minutes | **START TO FINISH:** 50 Minutes | **8 servings**

3 cups shredded deli rotisserie chicken (from 2-lb chicken)

1 package (.58 oz) chicken taco seasoning mix

1 can (15 oz) black beans, rinsed, drained

1 can (4 oz) chopped green chiles

1 cup frozen whole kernel corn (from 12-oz package)

¼ cup water

1 can Pillsbury Grands! Flaky Layers refrigerated buttermilk biscuits (8 biscuits)

1 package (8 oz) shredded Mexican cheese blend (2 cups)

1. Heat oven to 375°F. Spray 13x9-inch (3-quart) glass baking dish with cooking spray.

2. In 12-inch nonstick skillet, cook chicken, taco seasoning, black beans, green chiles, corn and water over medium heat 5 to 6 minutes, stirring frequently, until thoroughly heated. Remove from heat.

3. Separate dough into 8 biscuits; cut each into 8 pieces. Add biscuit pieces and 1 cup of the cheese to the chicken mixture and stir gently until pieces are coated. Spread evenly in baking dish.

4. Bake 18 to 23 minutes or until biscuits are golden brown and no longer doughy in center.

5. Sprinkle with remaining 1 cup cheese. Bake 3 to 4 minutes longer or until cheese is melted.

1 Serving: Calories 450; Total Fat 19g (Saturated Fat 9g, Trans Fat 0g); Cholesterol 70mg; Sodium 1210mg; Total Carbohydrate 42g (Dietary Fiber 5g); Protein 28g **Exchanges:** 1½ Starch, 1½ Other Carbohydrate, 2½ Lean Meat, 1 High-Fat Meat, ½ Fat **Carbohydrate Choices:** 3

KITCHEN SECRET

◆ If you can't find the chicken taco seasoning mix, regular taco seasoning mix works just as well.

SERVE IT UP

◆ Serve with a fresh tossed salad and carrot and celery sticks and cucumber slices.

◆ Serve this main dish with your favorite salsa.

ADD A GARNISH

◆ If you like, top each serving with shredded lettuce, chopped tomatoes, sour cream or sliced green onions.

CHICKEN-VEGGIE RANCH BUBBLE-UP

PREP TIME: 20 Minutes | **START TO FINISH:** 50 Minutes | **6 servings**

1 tablespoon vegetable oil

1 lb boneless skinless chicken breasts, cut into ¾ inch pieces

1 bag (14 oz) frozen broccoli stir-fry vegetables

1¼ cups regular or light prepared ranch dressing

1½ cups shredded Italian cheese blend (6 oz)

1 can Pillsbury Grands! Flaky Layers refrigerated buttermilk biscuits (8 biscuits)

1 package (0.4 oz) ranch dressing mix (buttermilk recipe)

1 Heat oven to 350°F. Spray 13x9-inch pan with cooking spray.

2 In 12-inch nonstick skillet, heat oil over medium-high heat. Add chicken and vegetables; cook 8 to 10 minutes, stirring occasionally, until chicken is no longer pink in center. Stir in prepared dressing; stir in 1 cup of the cheese. Spoon into baking dish.

3 Meanwhile, separate dough into 8 biscuits; cut each into 8 pieces. Place pieces in 1-gallon resealable food-storage plastic bag; add dry dressing mix and remaining ½ cup cheese. Seal bag; shake to coat biscuit pieces. Arrange pieces evenly over chicken mixture.

4 Bake 28 to 30 minutes or until golden brown and biscuits are no longer doughy in center.

1 Serving: Calories 670; Total Fat 42g (Saturated Fat 12g, Trans Fat 0g); Cholesterol 85mg; Sodium 1430mg; Total Carbohydrate 43g (Dietary Fiber 2g); Protein 31g **Exchanges:** 1 Starch, 1½ Other Carbohydrate, 1 Vegetable, 2½ Lean Meat, 1 High-Fat Meat, 5 Fat **Carbohydrate Choices:** 3

KITCHEN SECRET

◆ Check to see if the biscuit topping is cooked all the way through by carefully lifting one of the biscuit bubbles with a fork or knife. If it still looks doughy, bake it a few minutes longer.

SERVE IT UP

◆ Sliced apples, orange slices or other fresh fruit make a nice accompaniment to this family-friendly main dish.

NACHO MEATBALL BAKE

PREP TIME: 15 Minutes | **START TO FINISH:** 1 Hour 5 Minutes | **8 servings**

1   can Pillsbury Grands! Flaky Layers refrigerated buttermilk biscuits

1   jar (15 oz) salsa queso cheese dip

2   tablespoons chopped fresh cilantro

1   lb refrigerated or thawed frozen cooked beef meatballs, cut in half (about 22)

1   can (14.5 oz) diced tomatoes, drained

1. Heat oven to 375°F. Spray 13x9-inch (3-quart) glass baking dish with cooking spray.

2. Separate dough into 8 biscuits; cut each biscuit into 8 pieces. Place pieces in baking dish. Drizzle with ¾ cup of the queso dip; toss to coat biscuit pieces. Sprinkle with 1 tablespoon of the cilantro. Arrange meatballs and tomatoes over biscuits; drizzle with remaining queso dip.

3. Bake 35 to 40 minutes or until biscuits are deep golden brown and no longer doughy in center. Sprinkle with remaining 1 tablespoon cilantro. Let stand 10 minutes.

1 Serving: Calories 400; Total Fat 19g (Saturated Fat 7g, Trans Fat 0g); Cholesterol 60mg; Sodium 1300mg; Total Carbohydrate 39g (Dietary Fiber 1g); Protein 17g **Exchanges:** 1 Starch, 1½ Other Carbohydrate, ½ Vegetable, 2 Lean Meat, 2½ Fat **Carbohydrate Choices:** 2½

KITCHEN SECRETS

◆ This family-pleasing meal uses frozen or refrigerated meatballs, but you can use your own homemade meatballs as well.

◆ Cut the biscuits quickly by stacking two at a time and cutting them into 8 pieces.

ADD A GARNISH

◆ Top each serving with chopped tomato and avocado—yum!

CHICKEN-BACON CAESAR BUBBLE-UP BAKE

PREP TIME: 10 Minutes | **START TO FINISH:** 50 Minutes | **8 servings**

- 1 container (8 oz) garlic & herbs spreadable cheese
- ½ cup Caesar dressing
- ¼ cup water
- ¼ teaspoon pepper
- 1 can Pillsbury Grands! Flaky Layers refrigerated buttermilk biscuits (8 biscuits)
- 2 cups chopped deli rotisserie chicken (from 2-lb chicken)
- ¾ cup chopped cooked bacon
- 2 cups coarsely chopped fresh spinach
- 2 cups shredded Italian cheese blend (8 oz)

1. Heat oven to 350°F. Spray 13x9-inch (3-quart) glass baking dish with cooking spray.

2. In large bowl, mix spreadable cheese, dressing, water and pepper with whisk. Separate dough into 8 biscuits; cut each into 6 pieces. Add pieces to bowl and mix until incorporated.

3. Add chicken, half of the bacon, the spinach, and 1 cup of the cheese blend to biscuit mixture; fold in until mixed well.

4. Spoon mixture into baking dish; top with remaining 1 cup cheese blend and the remaining bacon.

5. Bake 33 to 37 minutes or until biscuits are deep golden brown and no longer doughy in center.

1 Serving: Calories 520; Total Fat 34g (Saturated Fat 14g, Trans Fat 0.5g); Cholesterol 95mg; Sodium 1260mg; Total Carbohydrate 29g (Dietary Fiber 0g); Protein 24g **Exchanges:** 2 Starch, 1 Very Lean Meat, 1½ High-Fat Meat, 4 Fat **Carbohydrate Choices:** 2

SERVE IT UP

◆ A fresh Caesar salad and favorite cooked vegetable make great additions to this meal.

ADD A GARNISH

◆ Top with sliced green onions or shredded Parmesan cheese.

BACON, EGG AND CHEESE BRUNCH RING

PREP TIME: 30 Minutes | **START TO FINISH:** 55 Minutes | **8 servings**

4 slices bacon, cut in half crosswise

⅓ cup plus 1 tablespoon milk

4 eggs, slightly beaten

Salt and pepper, if desired

¼ cup chopped red bell pepper

1 can Pillsbury refrigerated crescent dinner rolls (8 rolls)

1 cup shredded Mexican cheese blend (4 oz)

KITCHEN SECRET

◆ If you prefer or if you can't find the Mexican cheese blend, make your own. Mix ½ cup each shredded mozzarella, shredded provolone, shredded Cheddar and grated Parmesan cheeses.

ADD A GARNISH

◆ Garnish each serving with chopped tomato, chopped fresh cilantro, green onions, sour cream or salsa.

1 Heat oven to 375°F. Line large cookie sheet with cooking parchment paper.

2 In 10-inch skillet, cook bacon over medium heat about 4 minutes, turning once, or until cooked but not crisp. (It will continue to cook in oven.) Set bacon aside; drain all except 2 teaspoons bacon drippings from skillet.

3 In medium bowl, beat ⅓ cup of the milk, the eggs, salt and pepper with fork or whisk until well mixed. Stir in bell pepper. Pour egg mixture into skillet. As mixture begins to set at bottom and side, gently lift cooked portions with metal spatula so that thin, uncooked portion can flow to bottom. Avoid constant stirring. As more egg sets, push it to the edge and place on top of already-set egg mixture. Cook 5 to 6 minutes or until eggs are thickened throughout but still moist.

4 Unroll dough; separate into 8 triangles. On cookie sheet, with shortest sides toward center, arrange triangles in star shape leaving a 4-inch circle in center. Dough will overlap. (Crescent dough points may hang over edge of cookie sheet.) Press overlapping dough to flatten.

5 Place 1 piece bacon on each triangle. Sprinkle ⅓ cup of the cheese onto widest part of dough. Spoon eggs over cheese. Sprinkle with ⅓ cup of the cheese. Pull points of triangles up over filling, tucking under bottom layer of dough to secure it and form ring. Repeat around ring until entire filling is enclosed (some filling will be visible). Carefully brush dough with remaining 1 tablespoon milk; sprinkle with remaining ⅓ cup cheese.

6 Bake 20 to 25 minutes or until deep golden brown. Cool 2 minutes. With broad spatula, carefully loosen ring from cookie sheet; slide onto serving platter.

1 Serving: Calories 220; Total Fat 15g (Saturated Fat 6g, Trans Fat 1.5g); Cholesterol 110mg; Sodium 440mg; Total Carbohydrate 12g (Dietary Fiber 0g); Protein 10g **Exchanges:** 1 Starch, ½ Medium-Fat Meat, ½ High-Fat Meat, 1½ Fat **Carbohydrate Choices:** 1

MINI CHICKEN POT PIES

PREP TIME: 20 Minutes | **START TO FINISH:** 55 Minutes | 8 pot pies

1   package (10 oz) frozen mixed vegetables, cooked

1   cup diced cooked chicken

1   can (10¾ oz) condensed cream of chicken soup

1   can Pillsbury Grands! Flaky Layers Original refrigerated biscuits (8 biscuits)

1   Heat oven to 375°F. Spray 8 regular-size muffin cups with cooking spray.

2   In medium bowl, combine vegetables, chicken and soup; mix well.

3   Separate dough into 8 biscuits; press each into 5½-inch round. Place 1 round in each muffin cup. Firmly press in bottom and up side, forming ¾-inch rim. Spoon a generous ⅓ cup chicken mixture into each cup. Pull edges of dough over filling toward center; pleat and pinch dough gently to hold in place.

4   Bake 25 to 30 minutes or until golden brown. Cool 1 minute; remove from pan.

1 Pot Pie: Calories 250; Total Fat 10g (Saturated Fat 3.5g, Trans Fat 0g); Cholesterol 20mg; Sodium 730mg; Total Carbohydrate 31g (Dietary Fiber 1g); Protein 10g **Exchanges:** 1 Starch, 1 Other Carbohydrate, 1 Very Lean Meat, 2 Fat **Carbohydrate Choices:** 2

KITCHEN SECRETS

◆ If your family loves cheese, sprinkle some shredded Cheddar cheese over each pot pie about 5 minutes before the end of the baking time.

◆ Substitute any frozen (cooked) vegetables you have on hand, such as broccoli, corn, peas or green beans, for the mixed vegetables.

MINI SHEPHERD'S POT PIES

PREP TIME: 40 Minutes | **START TO FINISH:** 1 Hour 5 Minutes | **12 pot pies**

1 box Pillsbury refrigerated pie crusts, softened as directed on box

½ lb lean (at least 80%) ground beef

1 small onion, chopped

4 teaspoons all-purpose flour

¾ cup beef-flavored broth (from 32-oz carton)

½ teaspoon salt

⅛ teaspoon pepper

1½ cups frozen mixed vegetables

1 package (24 oz) refrigerated mashed potatoes (about 3 cups)

1. Heat oven to 375°F. Unroll pie crusts. On lightly floured surface, roll or press each crust to 12-inch diameter. Using 4-inch round cutter, cut 6 rounds from each crust.

2. Gently press rounds floured side down in bottoms and up sides of 12 ungreased regular-size muffin cups. Bake 9 to 11 minutes or until lightly browned.

3. Meanwhile, in 12-inch nonstick skillet, cook beef and onion over medium-high heat about 5 minutes, stirring frequently, or until beef is thoroughly cooked; drain. Stir in flour until blended. Add broth, salt and pepper. Cook about 2 minutes longer or until mixture thickens. Stir in vegetables. Spoon about ¼ cup beef mixture into each muffin cup. Top each with slightly less than 2 tablespoons potatoes.

4. Bake 20 to 25 minutes or until potatoes are lightly browned.

1 Pot Pie: Calories 240; Total Fat 10g (Saturated Fat 4g, Trans Fat 0g); Cholesterol 20mg; Sodium 530mg; Total Carbohydrate 31g (Dietary Fiber 2g); Protein 5g **Exchanges:** 1½ Starch, ½ Other Carbohydrate, 2 Fat **Carbohydrate Choices:** 2

KITCHEN SECRETS

◆ If you don't have a 4-inch round cutter, find an item of similar size in your kitchen, such as a small plate or a coffee mug. Place it upside down on the dough and trace around it with a paring knife.

KITCHEN SECRETS

◆ You can make these pot pies ahead and bake when you're ready. Prepare pies as directed through step 3.

- **To freeze:** Wrap muffin pan in foil and freeze completely. Remove to labeled 1-gallon resealable freezer plastic bag, and freeze up to 3 months.

- **To bake:** Heat oven to 375°F. Remove desired number of pies from bag; place in muffin cups or ramekins that have been sprayed with cooking spray on cookie sheet. Loosely tent with foil that has been sprayed with cooking spray. Bake 20 minutes. Remove foil; bake 8 to 10 minutes longer or until instant-read thermometer inserted in center reads 165°F.

ADD A GARNISH

◆ Sprinkle with chopped parsley after baking.

CHICKEN ALFREDO PASTA POT PIES

PREP TIME: 20 Minutes | **START TO FINISH:** 55 Minutes | **8 pot pies**

1 cup uncooked penne pasta

2 cups chopped cooked chicken

1 jar (15 oz) Alfredo pasta sauce

1 box (9 oz) frozen chopped spinach, thawed, squeezed to drain

1 can Pillsbury Grands! Flaky Layers refrigerated buttermilk biscuits (8 biscuits)

½ cup shredded Parmesan cheese

1 Heat oven to 350°F. Cook and drain pasta as directed on package.

2 In large bowl, mix pasta, chicken, Alfredo pasta sauce and spinach. Separate dough into 8 biscuits; press each into 5½-inch round. Firmly press 1 round in bottom and up side of each of 8 ungreased jumbo muffin cups, forming ¼-inch rim. Fill with chicken mixture; sprinkle with cheese.

3 Bake 28 to 32 minutes or until golden brown. Cool 1 minute; remove from pan.

1 Pot Pie: Calories 570; Total Fat 28g (Saturated Fat 14g, Trans Fat 4g); Cholesterol 85mg; Sodium 990mg; Total Carbohydrate 54g (Dietary Fiber 2g); Protein 25g **Exchanges:** 3½ Starch, 2 Lean Meat, 4 Fat **Carbohydrate Choices:** 3½

CHEESY FLORENTINE BISCUIT CUPS

PREP TIME: 20 Minutes | **START TO FINISH:** 50 Minutes | 8 biscuit cups

2 tablespoons butter

1 box (9 oz) frozen chopped spinach

½ teaspoon salt

¼ teaspoon pepper

1 can Pillsbury Grands! Flaky Layers Original refrigerated biscuits (8 biscuits)

4 oz thick-cut slices Canadian bacon, cut into ¼ inch cubes

8 eggs

2 cups shredded mild Cheddar cheese (8 oz)

1 Heat oven to 350°F. Spray 8 jumbo muffin cups or 8 (6-oz) glass custard cups with cooking spray.

2 In 10-inch skillet, melt butter over medium heat. Stir in spinach, salt and pepper. Cook 5 to 7 minutes, stirring occasionally and breaking up spinach if necessary, until spinach is hot. Remove from heat; set aside.

3 Separate dough into 8 biscuits. Place 1 biscuit in each muffin cup, pressing dough three-fourths of the way up side of cup. Spoon heaping 1 tablespoon Canadian bacon into each cup; top with spinach mixture. Using finger or end of wooden spoon handle, make 1½-inch-wide indentation in center of each cup. Break 1 egg into each indentation; top with ¼ cup cheese (cups will be full). (If using custard cups, place on 15x10x1-inch pan.)

4 Bake 20 to 25 minutes or until centers feel firm when touched and biscuits are golden brown. Cool 5 minutes. Remove from pan to serving plates. Serve warm.

1 Biscuit Cup: Calories 420; Total Fat 25g (Saturated Fat 12g, Trans Fat 0g); Cholesterol 230mg; Sodium 1040mg; Total Carbohydrate 28g (Dietary Fiber 1g); Protein 20g **Exchanges:** 1 Starch, 1 Other Carbohydrate, 2½ Medium-Fat Meat, 2½ Fat **Carbohydrate Choices:** 2

KITCHEN SECRET

◆ You can substitute ¼ pound bacon, cut into pieces, cooked and drained, for the Canadian bacon.

TURKEY AND VEGGIE ALFREDO POT PIE

PREP TIME: 20 Minutes | **START TO FINISH:** 40 Minutes | 5 servings

1   bag (12 oz) frozen broccoli, carrots, cauliflower & cheese sauce

1   tablespoon butter

½   cup chopped onion

½   cup chopped red bell pepper

1   jar (15 oz) Alfredo pasta sauce

2   cups cubed cooked turkey

3   tablespoons chopped fresh basil leaves

¼   teaspoon freshly ground black pepper

2   cans Pillsbury Grands! Juniors Flaky Layers refrigerated buttermilk biscuits (5 biscuits each)

2   tablespoons shredded fresh Parmesan cheese

1   Heat oven to 375°F. Spray 8-inch square (2-quart) glass baking dish with cooking spray. Cook frozen vegetables as directed on bag for minimum time.

2   Meanwhile, in 10-inch nonstick skillet, melt butter over medium heat. Cook onion and bell pepper in butter about 5 minutes, stirring occasionally, until tender. Stir in Alfredo sauce, turkey, cooked vegetables with sauce, basil and black pepper. Cook, stirring constantly, until mixture is thoroughly heated and bubbly. Spoon into baking dish.

3   Separate dough into 10 biscuits; cut each in half crosswise. Arrange around edge of baking dish, overlapping slightly. Sprinkle with Parmesan cheese.

4   Bake 18 to 20 minutes or until biscuits are golden brown.

1 Serving: Calories 640; Total Fat 40g (Saturated Fat 22g, Trans Fat 1g); Cholesterol 145mg; Sodium 1250mg; Total Carbohydrate 45g (Dietary Fiber 2g); Protein 26g **Exchanges:** 1 Starch, 2 Other Carbohydrate, 3 Lean Meat, 6 Fat **Carbohydrate Choices:** 3

KITCHEN SECRETS

◆ If you have leftover chicken or deli rotisserie chicken on hand, you can use it instead of the turkey in this recipe.

◆ If you don't have fresh basil leaves, substitute 1 tablespoon dried basil leaves for the fresh ones.

BACON-CHEESE CHILES RELLENOS

PREP TIME: 25 Minutes | **START TO FINISH:** 40 Minutes | 16 chiles rellenos

4   jalapeño chiles (about
    3 inches long)

⅓   cup soft garlic-and-
    herbs cheese
    (from 5.2-oz container)

8   slices packaged precooked
    bacon (from 2.2-oz package),
    cut in half crosswise

1   can Pillsbury refrigerated
    crescent dinner rolls (8 rolls)

1   Heat oven to 375°F. Carefully remove stems from chiles; cut each in half lengthwise and again horizontally to make 4 pieces. Remove and discard seeds. Spoon about 1 teaspoon cheese into each chile quarter. Wrap 1 piece of bacon around each.

2   Unroll dough on cutting board; separate dough into 8 triangles. From center of longest side to opposite point, cut each triangle in half, making 16 triangles. Place 1 chile cheese side down on triangle. Fold one point of triangle over filling; fold two remaining points over first point. Place on ungreased cookie sheet.

3   Bake 12 to 15 minutes or until golden brown. Immediately remove from cookie sheet.

1 Chile Relleno: Calories 170; Total Fat 10g (Saturated Fat 4.5g, Trans Fat 0g); Cholesterol 15mg; Sodium 380mg; Total Carbohydrate 13g (Dietary Fiber 0g); Protein 5g **Exchanges:** 1 Starch, 2 Fat **Carbohydrate Choices:** 1

KITCHEN SECRET

◆ One can (4 ounces) whole green chiles, drained and cut into 16 pieces, can be substituted for the whole jalapeño chiles.

SERVE IT UP

◆ Chiles Rellenos can be served with salsa, cheese dip or sour cream. They are great for dinner or as an appetizer!

PIZZA CRUST HACKS

Try one of these irresistible crust treatments to wow your hungry clan!

PARMESAN CRUST *(bottom)*

Roll out classic pizza dough as directed on package. Brush with 2 tablespoons softened butter; sprinkle with ½ cup shredded Parmesan cheese. Prebake crust at 400°F 7 minutes. Top with your favorite toppings and bake 7 to 9 minutes longer.

SPICY GARLIC BUTTER—HERB PIZZA CRUST *(upper right)*

Roll out classic pizza dough as directed on package. Brush with 2 tablespoons softened butter; sprinkle with 1 tablespoon finely chopped garlic (roasted for more flavor), ½ teaspoon Italian seasoning and ¼ teaspoon red pepper flakes. Prebake crust at 400°F 7 minutes. Top with your favorite toppings and bake 7 to 9 minutes longer.

STUFFED-CRUST PIZZA CRUST
(upper left)

Arrange 7 (1-ounce) string cheese sticks to form a circle on the crust about ½ inch from edge. Fold edge of dough over cheese; pinch firmly to seal. Top with your favorite toppings and bake at 425°F 12 to 16 minutes or until crust is deep golden brown and cheese is melted.

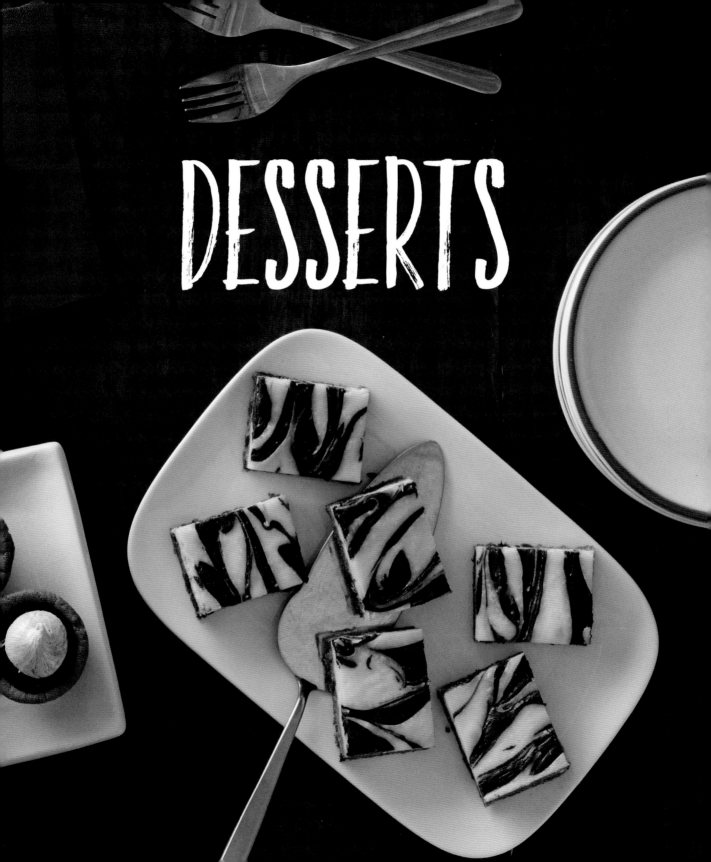

DESSERTS

EASY-DIPPED SUGAR COOKIE STICKS

PREP TIME: 30 Minutes | **START TO FINISH:** 1 Hour 45 Minutes | **2½ dozen cookies**

1 roll (16.5 oz) Pillsbury refrigerated sugar cookies

¼ cup all-purpose flour

8 oz white candy coating (almond bark) (from 20-oz package), cut into pieces

2 tablespoons red, green or white decorator sugar crystals or sprinkles

1 Heat oven to 350°F. Let cookie dough stand at room temperature 10 minutes to soften. Line large cookie sheet with cooking parchment paper.

2 In large bowl, break up cookie dough. Stir or knead in flour until well blended. Place cookie dough on cookie sheet; press into 15x8-inch rectangle. With pizza cutter or sharp knife, cut dough into 30 (4x1-inch) sticks (do not separate).

3 Bake 12 to 15 minutes or until edges are light golden brown. Cool 2 minutes. Cut into 30 sticks with knife. Cool 1 minute; remove from cookie sheet to cooling rack, separating into cookie sticks. Cool completely, about 20 minutes.

4 Meanwhile, in small bowl, melt candy coating as directed on package. Dip one end of each stick into candy coating; dip or sprinkle with sugar crystals.

1 Cookie: Calories 110; Total Fat 5g (Saturated Fat 2.5g, Trans Fat 0g); Cholesterol 0mg; Sodium 55mg; Total Carbohydrate 15g (Dietary Fiber 0g); Protein 0g **Exchanges:** 1 Other Carbohydrate, 1 Fat **Carbohydrate Choices:** 1

KITCHEN SECRET

◆ Substitute chocolate candy coating for the vanilla.

KITCHEN HACK

PERFECT COOKIES

For nicely rounded, same-size cookies, use an ice-cream scoop to portion your cookie dough onto the cookie sheet. Use one with the capacity equal to what is called for in the recipe.

SANTA'S BELLY COOKIES

PREP TIME: 30 Minutes | **START TO FINISH:** 1 Hour 5 Minutes | **2 dozen cookies**

1 package Pillsbury Ready to Bake!™ refrigerated sugar cookies (24 cookies)

24 large marshmallows

1 container (16 oz) vanilla creamy ready-to-spread frosting

Red, yellow and black gel food colors

48 white vanilla baking chips

1 Heat oven to 350°F. On ungreased cookie sheet, place cookies 2 inches apart.

2 Bake 10 to 12 minutes or until edges are light golden brown.

3 Remove from oven; top each cookie with 1 marshmallow. Bake 1 to 2 minutes longer or until slightly softened.

4 Remove cookies from cookie sheets to cooling racks; cool completely, about 20 minutes.

5 Meanwhile, spoon frosting into 3 small bowls, using 1¼ cups to make red frosting, ¼ cup for yellow frosting and ¼ cup for black frosting. Add food color to each, and mix to get desired colors.

6 Frost and decorate cookies to look like Santa's belly, using photo as a guide. Store cookies in a covered container.

1 Cookie: Calories 180; Total Fat 6g (Saturated Fat 3g, Trans Fat 0g); Cholesterol 0mg; Sodium 95mg; Total Carbohydrate 30g (Dietary Fiber 0g); Protein 0g **Exchanges:** 2 Other Carbohydrate, 1 Fat **Carbohydrate Choices:** 2

KITCHEN SECRETS

◆ As an alternative to yellow and black frosting, try using colorful candies (black licorice, gumdrops, mini candy-coated chocolates) to customize Santa's belt and buckle.

◆ It helps to flatten the marshmallows slightly before frosting if they seem too puffy.

PUPPY LOVE COOKIES

PREP TIME: 35 Minutes | START TO FINISH: 1 Hour 20 Minutes | 1 dozen cookies

1 package Pillsbury Ready to Bake! refrigerated chocolate chip cookies (24 cookies)

¾ cup fluffy white whipped ready-to-spread frosting (from 12-oz container)

⅓ cup chocolate creamy ready-to-spread frosting (from 16-oz container)

24 large pink and red heart-shaped candy decors

1 Heat oven to 350°F. On each of 2 ungreased cookie sheets, place 6 cookies 3 inches apart for puppy faces. Cut remaining 12 cookies in half; place 2 halves on sides of each whole cookie for ears.

2 Bake 9 to 13 minutes or until golden brown. Cool 2 minutes; remove from cookie sheets to cooling racks. Cool completely, about 15 minutes.

3 Frost puppy face with white frosting and ears with chocolate frosting. Decorate each puppy with heart shapes for eyes and nose. Spoon remaining chocolate frosting into small resealable food-storage plastic bag. Cut off tiny corner. Squeeze bag to pipe mouth onto each face. Store loosely covered.

1 Cookie: Calories 270; Total Fat 12g (Saturated Fat 4.5g, Trans Fat 1g); Cholesterol 0mg; Sodium 160mg; Total Carbohydrate 41g (Dietary Fiber 0g); Protein 1g **Exchanges:** ½ Starch, 2 Other Carbohydrate, 2½ Fat **Carbohydrate Choices:** 3

KITCHEN SECRETS

◆ You can substitute Pillsbury Ready to Bake! sugar cookies for the chocolate chip.

◆ Sprinkle ears with chocolate sprinkles to add texture.

KITCHEN HACK

TOASTING COCONUT

Place ¼ to ½ cup coconut in a glass pie plate. Microwave 1½ to 2 minutes, stirring every 30 seconds, until golden brown.

FROSTED RED VELVET SUGAR COOKIES

PREP TIME: 20 Minutes | **START TO FINISH:** 1 Hour 5 Minutes | **2 dozen cookies**

1   roll (16.5 oz) Pillsbury refrigerated sugar cookies

3   oz cream cheese, softened (from 8-oz package)

½   cup unsweetened baking cocoa

1   tablespoon red gel food color

1¼   cups marshmallow creme (from 7-oz jar)

½   cup butter, softened

1¼   cups powdered sugar

1   Heat oven to 350°F. In large bowl, stir cookie dough, cream cheese, cocoa and food color until well blended. Shape dough into 24 (1¼-inch) balls. Place balls 2 inches apart on ungreased cookie sheet. Using bottom of drinking glass, flatten balls to 1½-inch rounds.

2   Bake 10 to 13 minutes or until edges are set. Cool 1 minute; remove from cookie sheet to cooling racks. Cool completely, about 20 minutes.

3   Meanwhile, in large bowl, beat marshmallow creme and butter with electric mixer on medium speed until well blended. Beat in powdered sugar until smooth.

4   Spread frosting on cookies. Store in airtight container.

1 Cookie: Calories 180; Total Fat 9g (Saturated Fat 4g, Trans Fat 0g); Cholesterol 15mg; Sodium 115mg; Total Carbohydrate 26g (Dietary Fiber 0g); Protein 1g **Exchanges:** 1½ Other Carbohydrate, 2 Fat **Carbohydrate Choices:** 2

KITCHEN SECRETS

◆ No marshmallow creme? You can substitute 1 cup purchased vanilla frosting for the marshmallow creme mixture.

◆ If you don't have gel food color, substitute 1 tablespoon red liquid food color.

KITCHEN HACK

QUICK DECORATING

Spoon frosting or whipped cream into a resealable food-storage plastic bag. Seal the bag, removing any air. Cut off a small corner of the bag. Squeeze bag to pipe or drizzle the contents over quick breads, muffins, cakes or cupcakes.

Clockwise from top:
Quick Apple Pie Cups
(page 217)
Lemon Cookie and
Raspberry Yogurt Pops (right)
S'mores Layer Bars
(page 216)

LEMON COOKIE AND RASPBERRY YOGURT POPS

PREP TIME: 25 Minutes | **START TO FINISH:** 3 Hours 15 Minutes | 6 pops

1   roll (16.5 oz) Pillsbury refrigerated sugar cookies

2   teaspoons grated lemon peel

1½   cups whole-milk plain Greek yogurt

⅓   cup lemon curd (from 10-oz jar)

1   tablespoon honey

1   container (6 oz) fresh raspberries (about 1½ cups)

½   cup chopped slivered almonds, toasted

6   (5 oz) paper cups

6   craft sticks

1. Heat oven to 350°F. In medium bowl, mix cookie dough and 1 teaspoon of the lemon peel with spoon, or knead with hands, until well mixed. Shape dough into 26 (1 inch) balls. Place balls 1 inch apart on large ungreased cookie sheet.

2. Bake 11 to 14 minutes or until light golden brown around edges. Cool 1 minute; remove from cookie sheet to cooling rack. Cool completely, about 20 minutes.

3. Meanwhile, in medium bowl, combine yogurt, lemon curd, honey and remaining 1 teaspoon lemon peel until well mixed.

4. In 1-gallon resealable food-storage plastic bag, crush 10 of the cookies with rolling pin or meat mallet until coarsely crushed. Set aside. Reserve remaining cookies for another use.

5. To make pops: In each cup, layer 1 tablespoon cookie crumbs, 1 teaspoon almonds; top with 3 tablespoons of the yogurt mixture. Repeat with cookie crumbs and almonds; top with 3 or 4 raspberries and 3 tablespoons yogurt mixture. Repeat with cookie crumbs and almonds; top with 3 or 4 raspberries, pressing lightly.

6. Place cups in 13x9-inch pan. Insert craft stick into center of each cup. Freeze until firm, about 2 hours. Let stand at room temperature 15 minutes before serving. Remove paper cups.

1 Pop: Calories 530; Total Fat 25g (Saturated Fat 9g, Trans Fat 0g); Cholesterol 45mg; Sodium 300mg; Total Carbohydrate 69g (Dietary Fiber 3g); Protein 7g **Exchanges:** 1 Starch, ½ Fruit, 3 Other Carbohydrate, ½ Very Lean Meat, 5 Fat **Carbohydrate Choices:** 4½

KITCHEN SECRETS

◆ For easy removal of paper cups, cut a small slit in edge of cup with a scissors and then rip cup away from pop.

◆ To toast almonds, spread evenly on cookie sheet. Bake at 350°F 8 to 10 minutes, stirring occasionally, or until golden brown.

S'MORES LAYER BARS

PREP TIME: 25 Minutes | START TO FINISH: 3 Hours | 24 bars

1 roll (16.5 oz) Pillsbury refrigerated sugar cookies

1 cup crushed graham cracker crumbs (14 squares)

1 can (14 oz) sweetened condensed milk (not evaporated)

1 bag (12 oz) semisweet chocolate chips

1 jar (7 oz) marshmallow creme

2 cups miniature marshmallows

1 Heat oven to 350°F. Spray 13x9-inch pan with cooking spray.

2 In large bowl, break up cookie dough. Add graham cracker crumbs and knead until well mixed. Reserve ¾ cup dough mixture for topping. Press remaining dough mixture evenly into pan to form crust; set aside.

3 In 2-quart saucepan, stir together condensed milk and 1¼ cups of the chocolate chips. Heat over low heat, stirring occasionally, until chocolate is melted. Pour evenly over crust. Spoon marshmallow creme evenly over chocolate. Using a knife, cut marshmallow mixture through chocolate mixture in S-shaped curves in one continuous motion. Sprinkle reserved dough mixture evenly over top.

4 Bake 20 to 30 minutes or until bars are set and toothpick inserted in center comes out clean. Set oven control to broil.

5 Immediately sprinkle remaining chocolate chips and the marshmallows over warm bars.

6 Broil with top 4 to 5 inches from heat 30 to 45 seconds or until marshmallows are golden brown. (Watch carefully; marshmallows will brown quickly.) Cool on wire rack 1 hour. Refrigerate uncovered until completely cool, about 1 hour. Cut into 6 rows by 4 rows using sharp knife.

1 Bar: Calories 270; Total Fat 9g (Saturated Fat 5g, Trans Fat 0g); Cholesterol 10mg; Sodium 110mg; Total Carbohydrate 43g (Dietary Fiber 1g); Protein 3g **Exchanges:** 1 Starch, 2 Other Carbohydrate, 1½ Fat **Carbohydrate Choices:** 3

KITCHEN SECRETS

To microwave chocolate mixture, in medium microwavable bowl, heat chips and condensed milk on High 1 minute; stir well. Heat in 15-second increments, stirring well, if needed, until mixture is smooth.

For ease in cutting bars, be sure to cool them completely. When marshmallow mixture begins sticking to knife during cutting, wipe knife clean with damp cloth before cutting more rows.

QUICK APPLE PIE CUPS

PREP TIME: 10 Minutes | **START TO FINISH:** 35 Minutes | 8 cups

1   can Pillsbury Flaky
    refrigerated cinnamon rolls
    with butter cream icing
    (8 rolls)

1⅓ cups more-fruit apple pie
    filling (from 21-oz can),
    coarsely chopped

1   Heat oven to 375°F. Spray 8 regular-size muffin cups with cooking spray.

2   Separate dough into 8 rolls; set icing aside. Press 1 roll into and up side of
    each muffin cup. Spoon 2 generous tablespoons pie filling into cup.

3   Bake 14 to 18 minutes or until golden brown. Cool 5 minutes in pan.

4   Transfer icing to small microwavable bowl. Microwave uncovered on Low
    (10%) 8 to 10 seconds or until thin enough to drizzle. Place rolls on serving
    plate; spoon icing over rolls. Serve warm.

1 Cup: Calories 210; Total Fat 7g (Saturated Fat 3g, Trans Fat 0g); Cholesterol 0mg; Sodium 350mg;
Total Carbohydrate 34g (Dietary Fiber 1g); Protein 2g **Exchanges:** ½ Starch, 1½ Other Carbohydrate, 1½ Fat
Carbohydrate Choices: 2

KITCHEN SECRETS

◆ Use a nonstick muffin pan for easiest removal.

◆ Use leftover apple pie filling as a topping over vanilla ice cream or on waffles
or pancakes.

KITCHEN HACK

TAME THE STRETCH

When working with unbaked pie crust, move them without stretching them by
gently folding them into quarters or rolling up loosely on a rolling pin. Unfold or
unroll into the pie plate or onto the filling.

STRAWBERRY-CHEESECAKE COOKIE BARS

PREP TIME: 20 Minutes | **START TO FINISH:** 3 Hours 20 Minutes | 18 bars

1 roll (16.5 oz) Pillsbury refrigerated sugar cookies

3 packages (8 oz each) cream cheese, softened

½ cup sugar

3 eggs

½ cup seedless strawberry or raspberry jam

1 Heat oven to 350°F. Press cookie dough evenly in bottom of ungreased 13x9-inch pan. (If dough is sticky, use floured fingers.)

2 In large bowl, beat cream cheese and sugar with electric mixer on medium speed until blended. Add eggs, one at a time, beating on low speed after each, just until blended. (Don't overbeat.) Spread cream cheese mixture over dough in pan.

3 Place jam in small resealable food-storage plastic bag; seal bag. Cut off small corner of bag. Squeeze jam onto cream cheese mixture in 5 thick lines the length of the pan.

4 Use knife to pull all jam lines from top to bottom through cream cheese mixture at 1-inch intervals.

5 Bake 55 to 60 minutes or until filling is set in center. Cool in pan on cooling rack 30 minutes. Cover loosely and refrigerate until chilled, at least 1 hour 30 minutes but no longer than 24 hours. Cut into 6 rows by 3 rows. Store covered in refrigerator.

1 Bar: Calories 300; Total Fat 18g (Saturated Fat 9g, Trans Fat 0g); Cholesterol 75mg; Sodium 220mg; Total Carbohydrate 29g (Dietary Fiber 0g); Protein 4g **Exchanges:** 1 Starch, 1 Other Carbohydrate, 3½ Fat **Carbohydrate Choices:** 2

KITCHEN SECRETS

◆ To soften jam, microwave 10 to 20 seconds before placing it in plastic bag.

◆ To easily remove dessert, line pan with foil, extending over sides of pan. Before cutting into bars, lift cheesecake from pan using foil handles.

◆ You can omit the fruit spread if you like and top with fresh-cut strawberries and blueberries.

◆ Serving a crowd? Cut these bars into smaller squares for mini cheesecake bites.

FLUFFERNUTTER COOKIE CUPS

PREP TIME: 30 Minutes | **START TO FINISH:** 1 Hour | **24 cups**

1   roll (16.5 oz) Pillsbury refrigerated peanut butter cookies

⅔   cup semisweet chocolate chips

⅓   cup heavy whipping cream

¼   cup powdered sugar

2   cups marshmallow creme (from two 7-oz jars)

⅔   cup creamy peanut butter

1. Heat oven to 350°F. Spray 24 mini muffin cups with cooking spray.

2. Cut cookie dough into 24 slices. Press 1 slice in bottom and up side of each muffin cup (sprinkle fingers with flour if necessary to prevent dough from sticking to fingers).

3. Bake 8 to 11 minutes or until edges are deep golden brown. Cool 5 minutes.

4. With end of handle of wooden spoon, make 2-inch indentation in each cup. Cool 15 minutes longer. Gently remove cookie cups by lifting with thin metal spatula or knife.

5. Meanwhile, in small microwavable bowl, microwave chocolate chips and whipping cream uncovered on High 30 to 45 seconds or until chocolate can be stirred smooth. Spoon about 1½ teaspoons chocolate mixture into each cookie cup. Refrigerate 15 minutes.

6. In medium bowl, gently stir powdered sugar into marshmallow creme. Fold in peanut butter just until marbled. Spoon marshmallow mixture into resealable food-storage plastic bag. Cut ¾ inch from one corner of bag. Squeeze bag to pipe marshmallow mixture into cookie cups. Serve immediately or loosely cover and refrigerate up to 1 day.

1 Cup: Calories 200; Total Fat 10g (Saturated Fat 3.5g, Trans Fat 0g); Cholesterol 5mg; Sodium 140mg; Total Carbohydrate 25g (Dietary Fiber 1g); Protein 3g **Exchanges:** 1 Starch, ½ Other Carbohydrate, 2 Fat **Carbohydrate Choices:** 1½

KITCHEN SECRET

◆ By gently combining the powdered sugar with the marshmallow creme and then stirring in the peanut butter, the texture remains light and fluffy. Overmixing reduces the fluff and makes it grainy.

ADD A GARNISH

◆ These cookies are lovely by themselves, but for an over-the-top indulgence, dress them up with a drizzle of chocolate-flavor syrup and sprinkle of chopped roasted peanuts.

EASY GOOEY S'MORES BARS

PREP TIME: 20 Minutes | **START TO FINISH:** 1 Hour 30 Minutes | 9 bars

1 roll (16.5 oz) Pillsbury refrigerated chocolate chip cookies

1 cup graham cracker crumbs

1 jar (7 oz) marshmallow creme

1 Heat oven to 350°F. Spray 8-inch square pan with cooking spray.

2 In large bowl, break up cookie dough. Stir or knead in ¾ cup of the graham cracker crumbs until well blended (reserve remaining crumbs). Press half of the dough evenly in bottom of pan to form crust. Bake 13 minutes.

3 Spoon marshmallow creme evenly over partially baked dough; sprinkle with remaining ¼ cup graham cracker crumbs. Crumble remaining cookie dough on top.

4 Bake 20 to 25 minutes longer or until golden brown. Cool on cooling rack 30 minutes. Cut into 3 rows by 3 rows. Serve warm or cool. Store in tightly covered container.

1 Bar: Calories 340; Total Fat 12g (Saturated Fat 4.5g, Trans Fat 0g); Cholesterol 0mg; Sodium 220mg; Total Carbohydrate 57g (Dietary Fiber 1g); Protein 1g **Exchanges:** 4 Other Carbohydrate, 2½ Fat **Carbohydrate Choices:** 4

KITCHEN SECRET

◆ To make your own graham cracker crumbs, place 16 graham cracker squares in food processor. Cover; process, using on-and-off pulses, until fine crumbs.

ADD A GARNISH

◆ For a more decadent bar, drizzle tops with chocolate-flavor syrup before serving.

KITCHEN HACK

SLICK MOVE

When spraying muffin cups for cupcakes or muffins, spray the top of the pan lightly as well as inside the cups so any batter that accidentally falls on top of the pan will slide right off when cleaned.

PEANUT BUTTER CUP–COOKIE DOUGH BROWNIES

PREP TIME: 15 Minutes | **START TO FINISH:** 2 Hours 15 Minutes | 24 brownies

1 roll (16.5 oz) Pillsbury refrigerated chocolate chip cookies

24 large chocolate-covered peanut butter cup candies (from two 9-oz packages), unwrapped

1 box (1 lb 6.25 oz) supreme original brownie mix

½ cup vegetable oil

¼ cup water

2 eggs

1 Heat oven to 350°F. Line 13x9-inch pan with foil, allowing foil to hang over sides of pan for easy removal after baking. Spray with cooking spray.

2 Press cookie dough evenly in bottom of pan. Top with single layer of peanut butter cups. Make brownie batter as directed on box, using oil, water and eggs. Spread batter on top of peanut butter cups.

3 Bake 35 to 40 minutes or until brownies are set around sides and toothpick inserted in center of brownies (not candies) comes out clean. Cool on cooling rack 20 minutes. Using foil as handles, remove brownies to cooling rack. Cool completely, about 1 hour. Cut into 6 rows by 4 rows.

1 Brownie: Calories 330; Total Fat 17g (Saturated Fat 5g, Trans Fat 1g); Cholesterol 10mg; Sodium 200mg; Total Carbohydrate 42g (Dietary Fiber 1g); Protein 3g **Exchanges:** ½ Starch, 2½ Other Carbohydrate, 3½ Fat **Carbohydrate Choices:** 3

KITCHEN SECRET

◆ Swap out the peanut butter cups for your favorite sandwich cookies.

KITCHEN HACK

BROWN SUGAR SUBSTITUTE

No brown sugar on hand? Substitute 1 cup granulated sugar plus 2 tablespoons molasses for 1 cup of brown sugar.

CHOCOLATE CHIP COOKIE-CHEESECAKE BARS

PREP TIME: 10 Minutes | **START TO FINISH:** 3 Hours 50 Minutes | 20 bars

1   roll (16.5 oz) Pillsbury refrigerated chocolate chip cookies

2   packages (8 oz each) cream cheese, softened

1   cup sugar

3   eggs

½   cup heavy whipping cream

1   container (5.3 oz) 100-calorie fat-free Greek vanilla yogurt

1   Heat oven to 325°F. Grease or spray 13x9-inch (3-quart) pan or baking dish with cooking spray. Press cookie dough evenly in bottom of pan. Bake 12 minutes.

2   Meanwhile, in large bowl, beat cream cheese and sugar with electric mixer on medium speed until fluffy. Add eggs, one at a time, scraping side of bowl after each. Add heavy cream and yogurt; beat until just mixed. Pour over cookie dough.

3   Bake 40 to 45 minutes or until set around edges and only slightly jiggly in center when shaken.

4   Turn oven off; open oven door 4 inches. Leave cheesecake in oven 20 minutes longer. Remove from oven; cool on cooling rack at room temperature 20 minutes. Loosely cover and refrigerate 1 to 2 hours or until completely cooled. Cut into 5 by 4 rows. Cover and refrigerate any remaining bars.

1 Bar: Calories 260; Total Fat 16g (Saturated Fat 8g, Trans Fat 0g); Cholesterol 65mg; Sodium 170mg; Total Carbohydrate 26g (Dietary Fiber 0g); Protein 4g **Exchanges:** 1½ Starch, 3 Fat **Carbohydrate Choices:** 2

KITCHEN SECRET

◆ Adding the eggs one at a time adds air to the batter while smoothing out the lumps for bars with the best texture.

ADD A GARNISH

◆ Want to dress up your bars for the dessert table? Serve with little bowls of cherries, whipped cream, caramel sauce and whatever other sweets you fancy!

◆ If you like, drizzle refrigerated bars with 2 tablespoons chocolate-flavor syrup before cutting.

CHOCOLATE-HAZELNUT SWIRLED CHEESECAKE BARS

PREP TIME: 15 Minutes | **START TO FINISH:** 3 Hours 40 Minutes | **32 bars**

1 package Pillsbury Ready to Bake! refrigerated chocolate chip cookies (24 cookies)

2 packages (8 oz each) cream cheese, softened

½ cup sugar

1 teaspoon vanilla

2 eggs

⅓ cup hazelnut spread with cocoa (from 13-oz jar)

1 Heat oven to 350°F. Place cookies in ungreased 13x9-inch pan. Press dough evenly in bottom of pan to form crust.

2 Bake 9 to 13 minutes or until light golden brown. Cool 10 minutes.

3 Meanwhile, in large bowl, beat cream cheese, sugar, vanilla and eggs with electric mixer on medium speed until smooth. Spread evenly over baked crust.

4 In small microwavable bowl, microwave hazelnut spread uncovered on High 10 to 20 seconds to soften. Drop teaspoonfuls of spread onto cream cheese mixture. With knife, carefully swirl spread into top of cream cheese mixture.

5 Bake 25 to 30 minutes longer or until filling is set. Cool on cooling rack 30 minutes. Loosely cover and refrigerate about 2 hours or until chilled. Cut into 8 rows by 4 rows. Store covered in refrigerator.

1 Bar: Calories 130; Total Fat 8g (Saturated Fat 4g, Trans Fat 0g); Cholesterol 30mg; Sodium 105mg; Total Carbohydrate 13g (Dietary Fiber 0g); Protein 1g **Exchanges:** ½ Starch, ½ Other Carbohydrate, 1½ Fat **Carbohydrate Choices:** 1

KITCHEN SECRETS

◆ Softening cream cheese is easy. Just microwave unwrapped cream cheese on microwavable plate uncovered on High 10 to 15 seconds.

◆ Substitute Pillsbury Ready to Bake! refrigerated sugar cookies for the chocolate chip cookies if you prefer.

Clockwise from upper left:
Caramelized Banana Pizza (right)
Easy Fruit Pizza (page 233)
Mango-Berry Fruit Pizza
(page 232)

CARAMELIZED BANANA PIZZA

PREP TIME: 20 Minutes | **START TO FINISH:** 35 Minutes | **12 servings**

1   can Pillsbury refrigerated crescent dough sheet

¼   cup caramel topping

4   ripe medium bananas, cut into ¾ inch slices (about 3 cups)

⅓   cup plus 1 tablespoon hazelnut spread with cocoa (from 13-oz jar)

2   tablespoons toasted sliced almonds

1 Heat oven to 375°F. Spray cookie sheet with cooking spray. Unroll dough onto cookie sheet; press into 12x9-inch rectangle.

2 Bake 10 to 13 minutes or until golden brown.

3 Meanwhile, in medium microwavable bowl, mix caramel topping and bananas. Microwave uncovered on High 2 minutes 30 seconds to 3 minutes, stirring after every minute, until bananas are softened and caramelized. Cool 10 minutes.

4 Spread ⅓ cup hazelnut spread onto warm crust. Spoon banana mixture on top.

5 In small microwavable bowl, microwave remaining 1 tablespoon hazelnut spread uncovered on High 10 to 30 seconds or until thin enough to drizzle. Drizzle over banana mixture; top with almonds. Serve slightly warm or at room temperature.

1 Serving: Calories 130; Total Fat 3g (Saturated Fat 1g, Trans Fat 0g); Cholesterol 0mg; Sodium 170mg; Total Carbohydrate 23g (Dietary Fiber 1g); Protein 2g **Exchanges:** 1 Starch, ½ Other Carbohydrate, ½ Fat **Carbohydrate Choices:** 1½

KITCHEN SECRETS

◆ Microwave ovens vary, so carefully watch to avoid burning or overcooking the caramel.

◆ You can find toasted, sliced almonds sold in packages as salad toppers at larger grocery stores.

◆ You can substitute 1 can Pillsbury refrigerated crescent dinner rolls (8 rolls) for the dough sheet. Unroll dough and firmly press perforations to seal. Continue as directed.

MANGO-BERRY FRUIT PIZZA

PREP TIME: 20 Minutes | START TO FINISH: 1 Hour | 16 servings

1 roll (16.5 oz) Pillsbury refrigerated chocolate chip cookies

1 package (8 oz) cream cheese, softened

1½ cups chopped peeled fresh mangoes (about 1 mango)

1 tablespoon sugar

½ teaspoon vanilla

1 cup fresh raspberries

1 cup fresh blueberries

¼ cup hot fudge topping

1. Heat oven to 350°F. Line large cookie sheet with cooking parchment paper. Break up cookie dough onto cookie sheet. Press dough evenly into 10x8-inch rectangle.

2. Bake 13 to 15 minutes or until deep golden brown. Cool completely on cooking rack, about 25 minutes.

3. Meanwhile, in food processor, combine cream cheese, ½ cup of the mango, the sugar and vanilla; process until almost smooth, about 20 seconds. Cover and refrigerate until ready to use.

4. Spread cream cheese mixture over crust to within ½ inch of edge. Arrange remaining mango and berries on cream cheese mixture. Heat hot fudge topping as directed on jar; drizzle over fruit. Cover and refrigerate any remaining pizza.

1 Serving: Calories 220; Total Fat 12g (Saturated Fat 6g, Trans Fat 0g); Cholesterol 15mg; Sodium 135mg; Total Carbohydrate 26g (Dietary Fiber 1g); Protein 2g **Exchanges:** 1 Starch, ½ Fruit, 2½ Fat **Carbohydrate Choices:** 2

KITCHEN SECRETS

◆ You can also serve this pizza with caramel topping instead of the hot fudge or a mixture of hot fudge topping and caramel topping.

◆ Substitute coarsely chopped fresh strawberries for the raspberries if you prefer.

EASY FRUIT PIZZA

PREP TIME: 20 Minutes | **START TO FINISH: 2 Hours 10 Minutes** | **12 servings**

1   roll (16.5 oz) Pillsbury refrigerated sugar cookies

1   package (8 oz) cream cheese, softened

⅓   cup sugar

½   teaspoon vanilla

2   kiwifruit, peeled, halved lengthwise and sliced

1   cup halved or quartered fresh strawberries

1   cup fresh or frozen blueberries

2   tablespoons apple jelly

1   Heat oven to 350°F. Spray 12-inch pizza pan with cooking spray. Break up cookie dough in pan; press dough evenly in bottom of pan.

2   Bake 12 to 16 minutes or until golden brown. Cool completely, about 30 minutes.

3   In small bowl, beat cream cheese, sugar and vanilla with electric mixer on medium speed until fluffy. Spread mixture over cooled crust. Arrange fruit over cream cheese. Stir jelly until smooth; spoon or brush over fruit. Refrigerate until chilled, at least 1 hour. Cut into wedges or squares. Cover and refrigerate any remaining pizza.

1 Serving: Calories 320; Total Fat 15g (Saturated Fat 6g, Trans Fat 2g); Cholesterol 35mg; Sodium 170mg; Total Carbohydrate 43g (Dietary Fiber 1g); Protein 3g **Exchanges:** 1 Starch, 2 Other Carbohydrate, 3 Fat **Carbohydrate Choices:** 3

KITCHEN SECRET

◆ For best results, keep the cookie dough very cold until you're ready to use it.

KITCHEN HACK

WHIPPING CREAM

Chill your bowl and beaters. Whip heavy whipping cream (half-and-half and light cream won't have enough fat to whip) until peaks stand upright when lifting the beaters.

DOUGHNUT ICE-CREAM SANDWICHES

PREP TIME: 30 Minutes | **START TO FINISH:** 30 Minutes | **4 ice-cream sandwiches**

Oil for frying

1 can Pillsbury refrigerated crescent dough sheet

½ cup sugar

1 teaspoon ground cinnamon

2 cups ice cream, any flavor

½ cup chocolate-flavor syrup

2 tablespoons sprinkles

1 In deep fat fryer or heavy saucepan, heat oil to 375°F.

2 While oil is heating, unroll dough on floured surface or piece of parchment paper. Using 2½-inch round cookie cutter or regular-size mason jar lid, cut 8 rounds from dough.

3 Fry rounds in hot oil about 2 minutes on each side or until lightly golden. Drain on paper towels.

4 In medium bowl, combine sugar and cinnamon. When doughnuts are cool enough to handle, toss in cinnamon-sugar to coat.

5 Top half of the doughnuts with large scoop of ice cream, about ¼ cup each. Top with chocolate-flavor syrup and sprinkles.

6 Place remaining doughnuts over ice cream and press down to form sandwich. Serve immediately, or freeze until ready to serve.

1 Ice-Cream Sandwich: Calories 660; Total Fat 27g (Saturated Fat 10g, Trans Fat 0g); Cholesterol 30mg; Sodium 530mg; Total Carbohydrate 97g (Dietary Fiber 2g); Protein 6g **Exchanges:** 1 Starch, 5 Other Carbohydrate, ½ Milk, 4½ Fat **Carbohydrate Choices:** 6½

KITCHEN SECRETS

◆ You can substitute caramel topping or your favorite ice-cream topping for the chocolate-flavor syrup if you like.

◆ Wrap leftover sandwiches individually in plastic wrap and place in resealable freezer plastic bag. Store in the freezer.

COOKIES AND CARAMEL ICE-CREAM PIE

PREP TIME: 15 Minutes | **START TO FINISH:** 2 Hours 45 Minutes | **8 servings**

1 Pillsbury refrigerated pie crust, softened as directed on box

4 cups vanilla ice cream, slightly softened

½ cup caramel topping

1 cup chopped creme-filled chocolate sandwich cookies

1 Heat oven to 450°F. Make pie crust as directed on box for One-Crust Baked Shell using 9-inch pie plate. Cool completely, about 20 minutes.

2 Spread 2 cups of the ice cream in cooled baked shell. Drizzle ¼ cup of the caramel topping over ice cream; sprinkle with ½ cup of the cookies. Repeat layers with remaining topping and cookies. Cover and freeze at least 2 hours before serving. Store in freezer.

1 Serving: Calories 380; Total Fat 17g (Saturated Fat 8g, Trans Fat 0g); Cholesterol 35mg; Sodium 330mg; Total Carbohydrate 54g (Dietary Fiber 1g); Protein 4g **Exchanges:** ½ Starch, 2½ Other Carbohydrate, ½ Milk, 2½ Fat **Carbohydrate Choices:** 3½

KITCHEN SECRETS

◆ You can use your favorite flavor of ice cream: chocolate chip, cookies and cream, peanut butter cup or fudge ripple.

◆ You can substitute 1 Pillsbury Pet-Ritz® Frozen Deep Dish Pie Crust (from 12-ounce package) for the refrigerated pie crust. Bake crust as directed on package for a baked shell; continue as directed.

KITCHEN HACK

SPRINKLING POWDERED SUGAR

Add a light dusting of powdered sugar to the tops of cakes, cookies, muffins and other desserts. Spoon a tablespoon of powdered sugar into a fine-mesh strainer or tea infuser, and tap edge with the spoon.

CINNAMON ROLL-WAFFLE ICE-CREAM SANDWICHES

PREP TIME: 30 Minutes | **START TO FINISH:** 30 Minutes | 5 ice-cream sandwiches

Vegetable oil

1 can Pillsbury Grands! Flaky Original cinnamon rolls with icing (5 rolls)

2½ cups ice cream, any variety, softened slightly

1. Heat Belgian-style waffle maker. Grease generously with oil. Separate dough into 5 rolls. Spoon icing into small resealable food-storage plastic bag; set aside.

2. Using serrated knife, cut each roll in half lengthwise; grease both sides with oil. Place 1 or 2 pieces at a time (depending on how many fit without touching) on waffle maker. Close waffle maker.

3. Bake 1 minute 30 seconds to 2 minutes or until cooked and golden brown. Using wooden kitchen utensil, carefully remove to cooling rack. Repeat with remaining pieces, greasing waffle maker and dough each time. Cool completely.

4. Using ice-cream scoop, place about ½ cup ice cream in center of 1 waffle for bottom, and top with another waffle. Cut off corner of icing bag, and pipe icing on top of each sandwich. Serve immediately

1 Ice-Cream Sandwich: Calories 520; Total Fat 27g (Saturated Fat 12g, Trans Fat 2g); Cholesterol 30mg; Sodium 580mg; Total Carbohydrate 64g (Dietary Fiber 1g); Protein 6g **Exchanges:** 2 Starch, 2½ Other Carbohydrate, 5 Fat **Carbohydrate Choices:** 4

KITCHEN SECRETS

◆ Be sure to grease the waffle maker between each batch of waffles to help prevent the rolls from sticking and burning.

◆ Cleanup is a breeze when you wrap a paper towel around the end of a wooden kitchen utensil, such as the wooden handle of a spatula. Push the paper towel through the cooled waffle grates to help clean up any residue from baking.

ADD A GARNISH

◆ Add a festive pop of color by topping these ice-cream sandwiches with colorful sprinkles and powdered sugar. You can also roll the edges in sprinkles before adding the icing.

SALTED CARAMEL–PUMPKIN PIE CRESCENTS

PREP TIME: 15 Minutes | **START TO FINISH:** 30 Minutes | **8 servings**

1 can Pillsbury refrigerated crescent dinner rolls (8 rolls)

FILLING

⅓ cup canned pumpkin (not pumpkin pie mix)

3 tablespoons sugar

2 tablespoons caramel topping

½ teaspoon pumpkin pie spice

TOPPING

2 teaspoons sugar

⅛ teaspoon pumpkin pie spice

4 teaspoons caramel topping

¼ teaspoon coarse sea salt

1 Heat oven to 375°F. Line large cookie sheet with cooking parchment paper. Separate dough into 8 triangles.

2 In small bowl, mix filling ingredients. Spread about 1 tablespoon pumpkin filling onto each triangle. Starting at shortest side of triangle, roll up loosely to opposite point. Place on cookie sheet.

3 In another small bowl, mix 2 teaspoons sugar and ⅛ teaspoon pumpkin pie spice. Sprinkle over filled rolls.

4 Bake 10 to 12 minutes or until golden brown. Cool 5 minutes. Drizzle rolls with caramel topping; sprinkle with salt. Serve warm or at room temperature.

1 Serving: Calories 150; Total Fat 5g (Saturated Fat 2g, Trans Fat 0g); Cholesterol 0mg; Sodium 310mg; Total Carbohydrate 24g (Dietary Fiber 0g); Protein 2g **Exchanges:** ½ Starch, 1 Other Carbohydrate, 1 Fat **Carbohydrate Choices:** 1½

KITCHEN SECRETS

◆ You can prepare the filling up to a day in advance and store covered in the refrigerator.

◆ You can prepare the rolls up to 2 hours in advance before baking and store covered with plastic wrap in the refrigerator.

KITCHEN HACK

PICK THE PLATE

Use heat-resistant glass pie plates to get the flakiest pie crusts.

STRAWBERRY CHEESECAKE CRESCENT ROLL-UPS

PREP TIME: 25 Minutes | **START TO FINISH:** 45 Minutes | **12 roll-ups**

1 can Pillsbury refrigerated crescent dough sheet

4 oz cream cheese (from 8-oz package)

2 tablespoons seedless strawberry jam

½ cup chopped fresh strawberries

2 teaspoons butter, melted

1 tablespoon sparkling sugar

1. Heat oven to 375°F. Line cookie sheet with cooking parchment paper.

2. Unroll dough on cutting board; cut into 12 rectangles. In small microwavable bowl, microwave cream cheese uncovered on High 20 seconds to soften. Spread about 2 teaspoons cream cheese over each rectangle to within ¼ inch of edge. Gently spread about ½ teaspoon jam over cream cheese. Place about 2 teaspoons strawberries in center of rectangle; spread slightly.

3. Starting with shortest side, roll up each rectangle and pinch seam to seal. Place on cookie sheet seam side down. Brush with butter and sprinkle with sugar.

4. Bake 12 to 15 minutes or until golden brown. Cool 2 minutes; remove from cookie sheet. Serve warm.

1 Roll-Up: Calories 110; Total Fat 6g (Saturated Fat 3g, Trans Fat 0g); Cholesterol 10mg; Sodium 190mg; Total Carbohydrate 13g (Dietary Fiber 0g); Protein 1g **Exchanges:** 1 Other Carbohydrate, 1 Fat **Carbohydrate Choices:** 1

KITCHEN SECRETS

◆ You can substitute 1 can Pillsbury refrigerated crescent dinner rolls (8 rolls) for the dough sheet. Unroll dough and press perforations to seal. Continue as directed.

◆ Sparkling sugar can be found in the baking aisle of your grocery store with the cake decorating products. If you don't have it, regular sugar will work.

VERY-BERRY CINNAMON ROLL PIE

PREP TIME: 30 Minutes | START TO FINISH: 4 Hours | 8 servings

1   Pillsbury refrigerated pie crust, softened as directed on box

¾   cup granulated sugar

⅓   cup cornstarch

3   cups sliced fresh strawberries (about 16 oz)

2   cups fresh raspberries (about 12 oz)

½   cup all-purpose flour

¼   cup packed brown sugar

2   tablespoons cold butter

1   can Pillsbury Grands! refrigerated cinnamon rolls with icing (5 rolls)

1   Heat oven to 400°F. Slowly and gently unroll crust in 9-inch pie plate. Press crust firmly against side and bottom. Fold excess crust under and press together to form thick crust edge; flute edge. Lightly crumple foil into balls about 2½ inches in diameter, and place on top of crust. Bake 5 minutes; cool completely on cooling rack.

2   In medium bowl, mix granulated sugar and cornstarch. Gently toss with berries; spoon into partially baked crust. In small bowl, combine flour and brown sugar. With fork or pastry blender, cut in butter until mixture looks like fine crumbs; sprinkle over filling.

3   Cover edge of pie with 2- to 3-inch-wide strip of foil. Bake 30 minutes; remove foil. Bake 10 to 15 minutes longer or until crust is golden brown and juices are bubbly. Remove to cooling rack; cool at least 2 hours but no longer than 12 hours.

4   Heat oven to 350°F. Line cookie sheet with cooking parchment paper. Separate dough into 5 rolls. Place 1 roll in center of cookie sheet. Unroll remaining 4 rolls; wrap each around the first roll on cookie sheet, working outward to make a giant cinnamon roll 7 to 8 inches in diameter. Bake 20 to 25 minutes or until top is golden brown. Remove to cooling rack; cool 20 minutes.

5   Carefully transfer roll to top of pie; drizzle with icing. Serve warm.

1 Serving: Calories 510; Total Fat 14g (Saturated Fat 6g, Trans Fat 0g); Cholesterol 15mg; Sodium 480mg; Total Carbohydrate 92g (Dietary Fiber 5g); Protein 4g **Exchanges:** 2 Starch, 1½ Fruit, 2½ Other Carbohydrate, 2½ Fat **Carbohydrate Choices:** 6

KITCHEN SECRET

◆ A pastry blender is a kitchen tool used to mix a solid fat into flour. You can use a fork or potato masher as well.

SERVE IT UP

◆ This pie really needs no extras, but if you like, serve with a scoop of vanilla or cinnamon ice cream.

CARAMEL APPLE–RASPBERRY SLAB PIE

PREP TIME: 35 Minutes | **START TO FINISH:** 3 Hours 15 Minutes | **15 servings**

1 box Pillsbury refrigerated pie crusts, softened as directed on box

FILLING

6 cups sliced peeled apples (3 or 4 medium)

1 cup packed brown sugar

3 tablespoons all-purpose flour

1 teaspoon ground cinnamon

1½ cups fresh raspberries (about 6 oz)

CRUMB TOPPING

1 cup all-purpose flour

½ cup packed brown sugar

½ cup old-fashioned or quick-cooking oats

½ cup cold butter, cut into small pieces

TOPPING

¼ cup caramel topping

1. Heat oven to 400°F. Remove pie crusts from pouches. On lightly floured surface, unroll and stack crusts one on top of the other. Roll into 17x12-inch rectangle.

2. Fit crust into ungreased 15x10x1-inch pan, pressing into corners. Fold extra crust even with edges of pan.

3. In large bowl, toss all filling ingredients except raspberries until well mixed. Add raspberries; toss gently just until coated with flour mixture. Spoon apple-raspberry mixture evenly into crust-lined pan.

4. In medium bowl, mix flour, brown sugar and oats. Cut in butter with fork or pastry blender until crumbly. Sprinkle evenly over apple-raspberry mixture.

5. Bake 32 to 38 minutes or until crust and crumb topping are golden brown. Cool 2 hours. Drizzle with caramel topping.

1 Serving: Calories 350; Total Fat 13g (Saturated Fat 7g, Trans Fat 0g); Cholesterol 20mg; Sodium 210mg; Total Carbohydrate 55g (Dietary Fiber 2g); Protein 2g **Exchanges:** 1 Starch, ½ Fruit, 2 Other Carbohydrate, 2½ Fat **Carbohydrate Choices:** 3½

KITCHEN SECRET

◆ Use baking apples such as Braeburn, Granny Smith or Gala to give the best flavor and texture to this homemade pie.

SERVE IT UP

◆ This pie is perfect for a crowd. For a potluck, you can serve it at room temperature or warm with whipped cream or ice cream.

CHERRY-ALMOND HAND PIES

PREP TIME: 15 Minutes | **START TO FINISH:** 40 Minutes | **12 pies**

1   box Pillsbury refrigerated pie crusts, softened as directed on box

1½ cups more-fruit cherry pie filling (from 21-oz can)

¼   cup sliced almonds

1   tablespoon milk

1   tablespoon coarse white sparkling sugar

1   Heat oven to 425°F. Line two large cookie sheets with cooking parchment paper. On lightly floured work surface, roll each pie crust into 13-inch round. Using 4½- to 5-inch round cutter, cut 4 rounds from each crust. Reroll remaining dough to make 4 more rounds.

2   In medium bowl, stir together pie filling and almonds; spoon mixture onto one side of each round to within ¼ inch of edge. Brush edge of round with water. Fold rounds in half; press edges with fork to seal. Place on cookie sheets.

3   Cut small slit into top of each pie to allow steam to escape. Brush with milk and sprinkle with sugar; press lightly.

4   Bake 18 to 23 minutes or until golden brown.

1 Pie: Calories 120; Total Fat 5g (Saturated Fat 2g, Trans Fat 0g); Cholesterol 0mg; Sodium 90mg; Total Carbohydrate 18g (Dietary Fiber 0g); Protein 1g **Exchanges:** 1 Other Carbohydrate, 1 Fat **Carbohydrate Choices:** 1

SERVE IT UP

◆ These cute pies are great as an on-the-go snack, packed in a lunch box or served with a scoop of ice cream on the side.

ADD A GARNISH

◆ Lightly press additional sliced almonds onto pies with sparkling sugar before baking if you like.

CHOCOLATE–PEANUT BUTTER COOKIE PIE

PREP TIME: 15 Minutes | **START TO FINISH:** 1 Hour 50 Minutes | **16 servings**

1   roll (16.5 oz) Pillsbury refrigerated chocolate chip cookies

3   cups powdered sugar

1   cup peanut butter

¼   cup water

2   tablespoons butter, softened

1   cup milk chocolate chips, melted

1   Heat oven to 350°F. In bottom of ungreased 10- or 9-inch springform pan, break up cookie dough. With floured fingers, press dough evenly in bottom of pan.

2   Bake 14 to 18 minutes or until golden brown. Cool 15 minutes.

3   In medium bowl, mix powdered sugar, peanut butter, water and butter until well blended. (If necessary, add additional water 1 teaspoon at a time until mixture is smooth.) Drop spoonfuls of mixture over baked cookie crust; spread evenly to cover crust.

4   Spread melted chocolate chips over peanut butter mixture. If desired, carefully swirl chocolate with fork. Refrigerate about 1 hour or until chocolate is set.

1 Serving: Calories 390; Total Fat 19g (Saturated Fat 6g, Trans Fat 1g); Cholesterol 10mg; Sodium 180mg; Total Carbohydrate 49g (Dietary Fiber 1g); Protein 6g **Exchanges:** 1 Starch, 2 Other Carbohydrate, ½ High-Fat Meat, 3 Fat **Carbohydrate Choices:** 3

ADD A GARNISH

◆ Garnish the pie with pecan halves for a pretty presentation before refrigerating.

KITCHEN HACK

NO SHRINKING

Keep your pie crust from shrinking in the pie plate by easing it into the pie plate without stretching (see Tame the Stretch on page 217). When making the edge decorative, either hook the pastry edge over the rim of the pie plate while fluting, or press the pastry edge with a fork or spoon to the rim of the pie plate to secure it.

LEMON-ICEBOX PIE FLAG

PREP TIME: 20 Minutes | **START TO FINISH:** 4 Hours 45 Minutes | **20 servings**

1   roll (16.5 oz) Pillsbury refrigerated sugar cookies

6   egg yolks

2   cans (14 oz each) sweetened condensed milk (not evaporated)

1   cup lemon juice

1   container (8 oz) frozen whipped topping, thawed

⅓   cup blueberries, patted dry

2   cups raspberries, patted dry

1. Heat oven to 350°F. Spray 13x9-inch (3-quart) glass baking dish with cooking spray. Press cookie dough in even layer in bottom and 1½ inches up sides of baking dish.

2. Bake 22 minutes. Cool 10 minutes.

3. Meanwhile, in large bowl, beat egg yolks with whisk. Add condensed milk; beat until combined. Add lemon juice; beat until thickened, about 2 minutes. Pour egg mixture into cookie crust.

4. Bake 20 to 25 minutes or until set on edges but slightly jiggly in center. Cool 30 minutes at room temperature, then refrigerate until firm, at least 2 hours but no longer than 8 hours.

5. Spread whipped topping over top. Arrange blueberries in top left corner to create blue field-of-stars section of flag. Make 6 red stripes with the raspberries. Carefully cover with plastic wrap; refrigerate at least 1 hour but no longer than 8 hours. Cut into 5 rows by 4 rows.

1 Serving: Calories 290; Total Fat 11g (Saturated Fat 6g, Trans Fat 1.5g); Cholesterol 70mg; Sodium 130mg; Total Carbohydrate 42g (Dietary Fiber 1g); Protein 5g **Exchanges:** 1 Starch, 2 Other Carbohydrate, 2 Fat **Carbohydrate Choices:** 3

KITCHEN SECRETS

◆ Use a sharp knife wiped clean with a wet towel to cut clean slices, and use a metal spatula or pie server to lift the crispy cookie bottom from the dish.

◆ Bottled lemon juice works great in this recipe, but for a tangier version, use fresh-squeezed lemon juice, and add a tablespoon of grated lemon peel to the egg mixture before baking.

PEACH–PECAN PIE BUBBLE-UP

PREP TIME: 20 Minutes | **START TO FINISH:** 1 Hour 5 Minutes | 8 servings

1 cup packed light brown sugar

½ cup light corn syrup

¼ cup butter, melted

3 eggs

1 teaspoon vanilla

3 cups sliced peeled peaches (about 2 large) or frozen sliced peaches, thawed, drained

1 cup chopped pecans

1 can Pillsbury Grands! Flaky Layers refrigerated buttermilk biscuits (8 biscuits)

1. Heat oven to 350°F. Spray 13x9-inch (3-quart) glass baking dish with cooking spray.

2. In large bowl, beat brown sugar, corn syrup, butter, eggs and vanilla with whisk until well mixed. Stir in peaches and pecans; set aside.

3. Separate dough into 8 biscuits; cut each into 6 pieces. Gently stir biscuit pieces into peach mixture. Pour evenly into baking dish.

4. Bake 30 to 35 minutes or until golden brown and biscuits are no longer doughy in center. Cover with foil during last 10 minutes of bake time to prevent overbrowning. Cool 10 minutes. Serve warm.

1 Serving: Calories 560; Total Fat 24g (Saturated Fat 8g, Trans Fat 0g); Cholesterol 85mg; Sodium 540mg; Total Carbohydrate 77g (Dietary Fiber 2g); Protein 8g **Exchanges:** 1 Starch, ½ Fruit, 3½ Other Carbohydrate, 1 High-Fat Meat, 3 Fat **Carbohydrate Choices:** 5

KITCHEN SECRET

◆ For a richer flavor, substitute dark brown sugar for the light brown sugar.

ADD A GARNISH

◆ Serve this bubble-up with whipped cream and a drizzle of your favorite caramel topping.

CHOCOLATE HAZELNUT–TOFFEE BREAD PUDDING WITH CANDIED BACON

PREP TIME: 30 Minutes | **START TO FINISH:** 2 Hours 20 Minutes | **16 servings**

8 slices bacon

1 cup toffee bits

2 cans Pillsbury refrigerated cinnamon rolls with cream cheese icing (8 rolls each)

3 cups heavy whipping cream

1 cup packed brown sugar

1 jar (13 oz) chocolate-flavored hazelnut spread

6 eggs

½ teaspoon salt

1 Heat oven to 375°F. Line 15x10-inch pan with sides with foil. Place wire rack on foil; spray with cooking spray. Arrange bacon in single layer on rack; sprinkle 1 tablespoon of the toffee bits over each slice.

2 Bake 20 to 25 minutes or until bacon is cooked through and toffee bits are slightly melted. Cool on rack 10 minutes; remove to paper towel-lined plate. Cool completely, about 10 minutes.

3 Meanwhile, bake cinnamon rolls as directed on can; set icing aside. Cool 5 minutes.

4 In 2-quart saucepan, heat 2 cups of the whipping cream, the brown sugar and hazelnut spread over medium heat 3 to 5 minutes, stirring constantly, until sugar is dissolved and spread is melted. Remove from heat; cool 10 minutes.

5 In large bowl, mix eggs and salt with whisk. Gradually add cooled cream mixture, beating with whisk until smooth and well blended.

6 Cut each roll into 16 pieces. Add pieces to egg mixture; gently toss to coat, lightly pressing pieces down to absorb some of the liquid. Stir ¼ cup of the toffee bits into egg mixture until blended.

7 Spray 13x9-inch (3-quart) glass baking dish with cooking spray. Spread bread mixture evenly into baking dish, pressing down slightly. Bake 35 to 45 minutes or until knife inserted in center comes out clean. Cool 20 minutes.

8 Chop bacon into small pieces; sprinkle evenly over bread pudding.

9 In large bowl, beat remaining 1 cup whipping cream with electric mixer on high speed 2 to 3 minutes or until soft peaks form. Add reserved icing; beat just until blended.

10 Serve whipped topping with warm bread pudding; sprinkle with remaining toffee bits. Store covered in refrigerator.

1 Serving: Calories 640; Total Fat 37g (Saturated Fat 19g, Trans Fat 1g); Cholesterol 145mg; Sodium 560mg; Total Carbohydrate 68g (Dietary Fiber 2g); Protein 8g **Exchanges:** 1 Starch, 3½ Other Carbohydrate, 1 High-Fat Meat, 5½ Fat **Carbohydrate Choices:** 4½

COOKIE DOUGH HACKS

Break out a 16.5-ounce roll of cookie dough and stir up some smiles!

COOKIE CUPS *(top)*

Shape tablespoonfuls of cookie dough into balls; place into greased mini muffin cups. Bake 10 to 12 minutes or until golden brown. With small spoon, gently press dough in center of each baked cookie to make shape of cup. Cool 10 minutes; remove to cooling rack. Cool completely. Gently remove from cups and fill with desired filling.

5-INGREDIENT PUMPKIN COOKIES *(left)*

Break up sugar cookie dough in medium bowl; beat in 2 tablespoons pumpkin pie spice and ½ cup canned pumpkin (not pumpkin pie mix) with electric mixer until well mixed. Drop dough by rounded tablespoonfuls 2 inches apart onto ungreased cookie sheet. Bake at 375°F 14 to 16 minutes. Cool on cookie sheet 5 minutes before removing to cooling rack. Mix 1 (8-ounce) package softened cream cheese with 1 cup powdered sugar; spread on cooled cookies.

SECRET-CENTER COOKIES *(right)*

For each cookie, shape 2 tablespoons cookie dough around 1 unwrapped miniature chocolate-covered peanut butter cup candy; roll into a ball. Place balls in regular-size muffin cups, lined with paper baking cups. Bake at 350°F 18 to 22 minutes. Microwave a few tablespoons of chocolate creamy ready-to-spread frosting in microwavable bowl 10 to 15 seconds on Medium (50% power) just until drizzling consistency. Drizzle over cooled cookies; let stand to set up chocolate.

PILLSBURY PRODUCT INDEX

BREADSTICKS

CINNAMON ROLLS

COOKIE DOUGH

CRESCENT ROLLS

FRENCH LOAF

PIE CRUSTS

PILLSBURY GRANDS!

PILLSBURY TOASTER STRUDEL

PIZZA CRUST

METRIC CONVERSION GUIDE

U.S. UNITS	CANADIAN METRIC	AUSTRALIAN METRIC
¼ teaspoon	1 mL	1 ml
½ teaspoon	2 mL	2 ml
1 teaspoon	5 mL	5 ml
1 tablespoon	15 mL	20 ml
¼ cup	50 mL	60 ml
⅓ cup	75 mL	80 ml
½ cup	125 mL	125 ml
⅔ cup	150 mL	170 ml
¾ cup	175 mL	190 ml
1 cup	250 mL	250 ml
1 quart	1 liter	1 liter
1½ quarts	1.5 liters	1.5 liters
2 quarts	2 liters	2 liters
2½ quarts	2.5 liters	2.5 liters
3 quarts	3 liters	3 liters
4 quarts	4 liters	4 liters

INCHES	CENTIMETERS
1	2.5
2	5.0
3	7.5
4	10.0
5	12.5
6	15.0
7	17.5
8	20.5
9	23.0
10	25.5
11	28.0
12	30.5
13	33.0

U.S. UNITS	CANADIAN METRIC	AUSTRALIAN METRIC
1 ounce	30 grams	30 grams
2 ounces	55 grams	60 grams
3 ounces	85 grams	90 grams
4 ounces (¼ pound)	115 grams	125 grams
8 ounces (½ pound)	225 grams	225 grams
16 ounces (1 pound)	455 grams	500 grams
1 pound	455 grams	0.5 kilogram

FAHRENHEIT	CELSIUS
32°	0°
212°	100°
250°	120°
275°	140°
300°	150°
325°	160°
350°	180°
375°	190°
400°	200°
425°	220°
450°	230°
475°	240°
500°	260°

Note: The recipes in this cookbook have not been developed or tested using metric measures. When converting recipes to metric, some variations in quality may be noted.

RECIPE TESTING AND CALCULATING NUTRITION INFORMATION

RECIPE TESTING:

- Large eggs and 2% milk were used unless otherwise indicated.

- Fat-free, low-fat, low-sodium or lite products were not used unless indicated.

- No nonstick cookware and bakeware were used unless otherwise indicated. No dark-colored, black or insulated bakeware was used.

- When a pan is specified, a metal pan was used; a baking dish or pie plate means ovenproof glass was used.

- An electric hand mixer was used for mixing only when mixer speeds are specified.

CALCULATING NUTRITION:

- The first ingredient was used wherever a choice is given, such as ⅓ cup sour cream or plain yogurt.

- The first amount was used wherever a range is given, such as 3- to 3½-pound whole chicken.

- The first serving number was used wherever a range is given, such as 4 to 6 servings.

- "If desired" ingredients were not included.

- Only the amount of a marinade or frying oil that is absorbed was included.

- Diabetic exchanges are not calculated in recipes containing uncooked alcohol, due to its effect on blood sugar levels.

INDEX

Page numbers in *italics* indicate illustrations

# indicates quick-prep recipes

• indicates 3-ingredient recipes

* indicates 5-ingredient recipes